YANKEES
ESSENTIAL

YANKEES ESSENTIAL

Everything You Need to Know to Be a Real Fan!

Howie Karpin

TRIUMPH
BOOKS

Library of Congress Cataloging-in-Publication Data

Karpin, Howie, 1954–
   Yankees essential : everything you need to know to be a real fan! / Howie Karpin.
      p. cm.
   ISBN-13: 978-1-57243-817-0
   ISBN-10: 1-57243-817-7
   1. New York Yankees (Baseball team)—Miscellanea. 2. New York Yankees (Baseball team)—History. 3. Baseball fans—United States—History I. Title.

GV875.N4K38 2007
796.357'64097471—dc22

                                        2006030302

This book is available in quantity at special discounts for your group or organization. For further information, contact:

Triumph Books
542 South Dearborn Street
Suite 750
Chicago, Illinois 60605
(312) 939-3330
Fax (312) 663-3557

Printed in U.S.A.
ISBN: 978-1-57243-817-0
Design by Patricia Frey
All photos courtesy of AP/Wide World Photos except where otherwise indicated

Contents

Foreword by Joe Torre vii

Acknowledgments ix

Introduction xiii

Let the Dynasty Begin 1

Dugout Generals 8

In 1934 Yankees Lost More Than Pennant Race 24

Joe DiMaggio: 56 More Than Just an Unbeatable Number 28

Lou Gehrig's Disease: Did Babe (not Ruth) See It Coming? 33

Mickey Mantle: Could He Have Been the Greatest? 37

Roger Maris: The Asterisk That Never Was 43

The End of an Era in the Bronx 48

"Chez Yankees": Yankees Would Play at Shea in
    1974 and 1975 53

Reggie's Three-Home-Run Night: Vindication 59

The Comeback 65

The Day the Captain Died 74

The Other M&M Boys: Two Great Yankees Who Never
    Grabbed the Ring 82

The Core 89

1995 Season: They're Back! 104

No-No's: Yankees Pitchers' No-Hitters 111

Subway Series: Yankees versus Mets 127

Bonded by Pinstripe Glory 135

Frozen in Time: Moments That Fueled a Rivalry 149

The Final Out 156

Let's Make a Deal: Best and Worst Trades in
   Yankees History 163

Strangest Regular-Season Games in Yankees History 172

The Stadium: A Field of Dreams Whose Dreams Have
   Been Fulfilled 179

Answers to Trivia Questions 186

New York Yankees All-Time Roster 188

Foreword

The New York Yankees. The name itself implies winning, class, and a sense of extreme pride and tradition.

An 18-year major league playing career and three previous major league managing jobs helped prepare me for what I was about to face when I was named the 31st manager of the New York Yankees in November 1995.

Little did I realize that in a relatively short time, I would be fortunate enough to be catapulted among those great names of the past that have won championships while wearing the uniform of the most successful franchise in baseball history.

The mystique of the Yankee pinstripes was everywhere. You didn't have to be a part of the team to realize what it was all about, but you could never fully grasp the "magic" of the Yankees until you put on the jersey that has come to represent winning and greatness.

Having grown up in Brooklyn during the 1950s, the Yankees were the hated rivals. Even though I was a New York Giants fan, the Yankees still broke my heart many, many times.

The year after Brooklyn finally won their elusive championship, I was fortunate to have a ticket for Game 5 of the 1956 Series and was in the stands at Yankee Stadium on the day that Don Larsen did not allow a single Dodger base runner.

During my tenure as the Yankees manager, I've been fortunate to experience the feeling of winning a championship, not just once, but multiple times.

Almost every Yankees fan has a working knowledge of their glorious history and it's also been well documented in numerous publications.

Beyond all the world championships are stories of what led up to those victories.

This book gives you a slightly different spin on Yankees history.

You will relive many memorable moments, ones that have become familiar throughout the years, but this book gives you a little more insight into those moments and memories.

This book also focuses on the latest championship run. Before I was lucky enough to manage a World Series team, I was always on the outside looking in. It's like when you're a kid and you see someone enjoying a hot fudge sundae; you get a little envious because you want one of those, too.

Well, that's how I felt when we won my first title, and the Yankees' 23rd, in 1996; I had finally gotten that hot fudge sundae.

It's been gratifying and an honor to manage the New York Yankees, and I take great pleasure in getting a chance to relive the storied history of this ballclub.

The glory that came before me, and the continued success that I have been lucky enough to be a part of, will make for some interesting reading sessions.

—Joe Torre

Acknowledgments

There's no way I can begin an acknowledgments page for my first book without thanking my wife, Kathy, and my two boys, Daniel and Jacob. They have been my rock over the years. My career would never have gotten to this point, and this book would never have been written, were it not for their love and support.

Many thanks to my sister, Carol, and her husband, Barry Shore, who have always supported me in whatever I've tried to do. Thank you to Wendy and Sharon, Carol and Barry's daughters, and their families.

Throughout my life and my career, I've made some relationships that I absolutely treasure. When I reflect on my professional career, I must begin with Bill Shannon. Bill, who's been a mentor to me and is the best official scorer in the business, was in my corner when the time was right for me to become an official scorer. Bill is a vault of sports knowledge with a strong emphasis on baseball. To know him, interact with him, and call him friend has been one of the real treats in my life.

Phyllis Merhige deserves a lot of credit for "going out on a limb" when she hired me to be an official scorer. I hope I've justified her faith in me.

Rick Cerrone has been the media director of the New York Yankees since 1996, but I've known him a lot longer than that. This dream became a reality with his help, not to mention Jason Zullo and the entire media relations staff.

Even though this is a Yankees book, I've got to thank Jay Horwitz, Ethan Wilson, and Shannon Dalton of the New York Mets media relations staff for their support when I work as a scorer over at Shea.

Among my media colleagues, I've known Mike Geffner since I began covering baseball, and he's been a huge help to me throughout the years. Our discussions are priceless. Thank you to Bob Rosen, Bob Waterman, John Lambobarda, and my softball playing buddies at the Elias Sports Bureau. Dave Freeman, Jordan Sprechman, Steve Torre, and Steve Cohen of Sirius Satellite Radio are just some of the friends I've made from working in the "biz" and the press box.

I was honored when Joe Torre agreed to write the foreword. He's headed to the Hall of Fame, but as far as the Karpin household is concerned, he's already there.

Jim Kaat was a terrific major league pitcher and an even better person. Getting to know him on a personal level the past few years is something I'll always feel good about.

There are some people over the years who, for one reason or another, have touched me more than others. People like Willie Randolph, the great Yankees second baseman, who now manages the Mets. Willie always treated me first class, and he gave me confidence in my abilities to do a job. We're still good friends today.

Thanks to Derek Jeter, Bernie Williams, Don Mattingly, Tino Martinez, Dave Winfield, Robin Ventura, Buck Showalter, John Flaherty, Billy Sample, John Sterling, Michael Kay, Ken Singleton, Al Leiter, and Pedro Martinez. The list goes on and on, and I wish I could mention them all. Their accomplishments within the boundaries of the sport of baseball fed the passion to write this book. These were people who took a little time to get to know me over the years, and I cherish all of that.

I also wanted to acknowledge Aaron Boone. His quotes from "Pinstripe Glory" were nearly two years after he hit his famous home run. He was a terrific interview.

Yankee Stadium has been like a second home, so I've made numerous friendships along the way, including Tony Morante, who is an expert on the stadium itself and was helpful with his information.

Bob Sheppard was already a huge part of my life. I've been lucky that my career has taken me to the intersection of respect and friendship when it comes to the greatest voice in the history of PA announcing.

There are those who work behind the scenes at the Stadium. Thank you Mike Bonner and the whole scoreboard crew. From Paul Cartier, who has not skipped a beat replacing a friend, the late Eddie Layton, to Matt, the electrician, to Bill Stimers in his familiar seat— it's been a great time in my life covering the Yankees for more than 25 years.

I can't complete the stadium side list without mentioning Eddie Lucas. Eddie, who is blind but always attends games, has been an inspiration to all he meets, including me. Maybe someone like Bill Menzel, who graciously plays the role of Eddie's eyes, can read this to him.

I must thank Dr. David Kaufman of Montefiore Hospital in the Bronx. Dr. Kaufman contributed his knowledge of ALS (Lou Gehrig's Disease) for the story on the Yankees great.

All the friends I've made over the years are special but some are closer to me than others. Friends like Jay Nadler, Mark Feinman, Lew Rose, Rick Goldfarb, and Tommy Tighe. Thank you to Rich Coutinho, Mike Mancuso, Bill Meth, Sweeny Murti, and the rest of the Metro Radio Sports Reporters Association. There have been many others, including Corey Friedman, Gregg Trachtenberg, Larry "Beany" Binenstock, Gary Axelbank, Gary Simon, Rich Mancuso, and Billy Altman, not to mention Warren Fidel and all of my softball-playing amigos from Croes Avenue. While I'm at it, my basketball-playing partners on the Bullets as well as Monty and Colin from Snapper.

It has been a pleasure to call Keith Olbermann a friend. Keith is a baseball nut like me, so I can appreciate his tremendous passion, knowledge, and historical perspective of the game.

I want to thank my print-media friends who have been helpful over the years, including Bob Herzog, Jay Greenberg, Wallace Matthews, John Dellapina, Frank Isola, Larry Brooks, Kevin Kernan, Bill Madden, Pete Caldera, Norm MacLean, Jack O'Connell, the late Bus Saidt, and a host of others.

I also need to thank Al Coqueran for his friendship and some of the pictures that you see within the book.

Many thanks to SABR (Society for American Baseball Research) for providing the research tools that I needed to write the book.

Yankees Essential became a reality because of longtime friend Ken Samelson. Ken was the one who got the ball rolling on this book because he put me in touch with Tom Bast of Triumph Books. I want to thank Tom for taking a chance on me. When I think of Ken Samelson and this project, I look at it like a rookie pitcher throwing to a veteran catcher. I was the rookie because it was my first book. Ken was the veteran backstop because he's been down the road to publication before, and he nursed me through the development of this book until its completion.

I would be remiss if I didn't mention my late mother and father, Ruth and Sid Karpin. I know they're still looking out for me and Carol. From my career to my personal history, you hold on to those relationships that are memorable in your life.

Introduction

This book is not the culmination of a long journey but one of the real fun stops along the way. The journey began when I was much younger, when my passion for baseball and the New York Yankees also began.

When I was a kid, the Yankees were a major part of my life, and 45 years later they still are.

I was always fascinated by the way a baseball game was broadcast and covered by the media. In 1978 I got a taste of the business. It was late September 1978 and I was a junior at Lehman College. The Yankees were embroiled in a memorable pennant race with the Red Sox, and Yankees shortstop Bucky Dent was scheduled to speak at the school. At the same time, my show on the college radio station would be on the air. If he finished in time, maybe we could get him on the show? Sure enough, through the help of some colleagues, there I was, sitting face to face with Bucky Dent.

Little did I realize that three days after that interview Bucky Dent would hit one of the most important home runs in the history of the New York Yankees to help beat the Red Sox.

I was hooked. From there it was a job at SportsPhone, which led to covering baseball games. It was like seventh heaven when I began to report on major league games. I had privileges that I could only dream about before. Things like access to the field and interacting with the players. Playing for the Lehman College baseball team had prepared me for my initial experience of being close to the majors.

Half my life has been spent covering baseball, and I've learned my lessons well. To this day, I still appreciate every moment that I spend at the ballpark as if it's my first time all over again.

For the past eight years, I've been an accredited official scorer, working Yankees and Mets games. I have always had a desire to be part of a major league game in any way, shape, or form possible. As an official scorer, I have fulfilled that desire.

All these experiences came into play as I put this book together. Researching the past brought me back to my carefree days. The act of recalling the great moments and uncovering some new facts surrounding these events was a labor of love.

I hope that I've succeeded in offering a little different perspective on the great history of the New York Yankees. There has been so much written and documented over the Yankees' history, but there's so much that has not been documented or put into print.

I hope you enjoy reading this book as much as I enjoyed writing it. Thank you.

—Howie Karpin

YANKEES
ESSENTIAL

Let the Dynasty Begin

In January 1903, the sale of the Baltimore Orioles to Frank Farrell and Bill Devery for $18,000 became the seed that sprouted a team called the New York Yankees.

Farrell had political connections but also ran saloons and gambling houses. Devery was a former New York City policeman, a link that many believe led to the adoption of the famous interlocking N-Y that has adorned the cap since 1909. Unfortunately, Devery was also linked to police corruption.

The New York franchise received approval to play in the American League in March. The team played their home games at Hilltop Park, which was located at 168th Street and Broadway. The site was built in a place known as Washington Heights because of its proximity to sea level, and thus the New York Highlanders were born.

The club's first skipper was a player/manager named Clark Griffith, who pitched and won 14 games. The Highlanders first game was played in Washington, a 3–1 loss to the Senators. Jack Chesbro was the starter and loser.

A day later, the Highlanders would have their first win as they beat Washington 7–2. Harry Howell was the first winning pitcher.

The dimensions from left field to right field showed how difficult it must have been to hit a home run. It was 365 feet to left field, an astounding 542 feet to center field, and right field was 400 feet away from home plate.

On April 30 the Highlanders would win their initial home game with a 6–2 victory over Washington. But the Highlanders would experience an up-and-down first season as they ended the campaign

1

Jack Chesbro was New York's first starting pitcher, taking the hill and losing 3–1 to Washington in the Highlanders' debut. Pictured is his Hall of Fame plaque; he was elected in 1946.

in fourth place with a 72–62 record, 17 games behind the American League champion Boston Pilgrims.

"Wee Willie" Keeler was the leading hitter at .312 while Herm McFarland led in home runs with five. At second base Jimmy Williams drove in a team-leading 82 runs. John Dwight Chesbro (a.k.a. "Happy Jack" to his friends) started 36 games and posted a 21–15 record with 33 complete games. The Hall of Fame right-hander tossed more than 324 innings and struck out 147 hitters while walking 74.

The 1904 season became a historic footnote because it involved the Highlanders and the New York Giants stoking the fires of an intra-city rivalry, plus the first ever cancellation of a World Series. (Another World Series was cancelled in 1994 over a labor dispute.)

"Wee Willie" Keeler led the Highlanders with a .312 batting average in their inaugural season.

The Giants were runaway winners in the National League with a 106–47 record, but in late July manager John McGraw and owner John T. Brush announced that they had no intention of playing a postseason series with the American League champions. The Highlanders were battling the Boston Pilgrims, the defending AL champs, for the pennant, and McGraw did not want to risk the embarrassment of losing to his crosstown rival.

McGraw's beef was with American League president Ban Johnson, whom he felt mistreated him when he was managing the Baltimore franchise. "There is nothing in the constitution or playing rules of the National League which requires its victorious club to submit its championship honors to a contest with a victorious club in a minor league," said McGraw. "When we clinch the National

League pennant, we'll be champions of the only real major league," added the Hall of Fame manager.

The bickering went back and forth as Johnson answered McGraw's claim of one credible major league. "No thoughtful patron of baseball can weigh seriously the wild vaporings of this discredited player who was canned from the American League," said Johnson.

Going into the final weekend, the Highlanders trailed first-place Boston by only a half game in the standings. But the Highlanders took over first place by a half game as Jack Chesbro won his 41st game (the all-time single-season record) in a 3–2 victory.

The Pilgrims swept a doubleheader from the Highlanders, 13–2 and 1–0, to move back into first place the next day—one and a half games up on New York.

The teams were scheduled for another twin bill on October 10, one that the Highlanders needed to sweep if they hoped to stay alive for the pennant.

The clubs split as the Pilgrims clinched the AL pennant with a 3–2 win in Game 1. The nightcap went to New York, 1–0, as they finished the season 92–59, one and a half games behind Boston.

The team known as the Highlanders would play for eight more seasons, finishing over .500 only two more times, in 1906 and 1910. Following a 76–76 finish in 1911, the Highlanders closed out their 1912 season and existence with a 50–102 mark.

New York snapped a nine-game losing streak on the final day of the season as they beat Washington 8–6 in the final game at Hilltop Park on October 5, 1912.

The Yankees pinstripes came into existence during that final season. The famous uniform debuted in the home opener on April 11.

The Yankees would abandon the pinstripes for the next two years, only to bring them back for good in 1915.

The interlocking N-Y also came into existence during the Highlanders tenure. As mentioned previously, rumor had it that the design came about as a result of Devery's background with the New York City Police

TRIVIA

Who was the last Yankees rookie pitcher to win five games after September 1?

Answers to the trivia questions are on pages 186–187.

By the NUMBERS

15—Number of Yankees uniform numbers that are retired (for 16 players)

No. 1 Billy Martin—Former World Series–winning second baseman and manager

No. 3 Babe Ruth—Considered by many to be the greatest player who ever lived

No. 4 Lou Gehrig—Played in an incredible 2,130 straight games

No. 5 Joe DiMaggio—Hit in a record 56 straight games in 1941

No. 7 Mickey Mantle—Greatest switch-hitter in baseball history

No. 8 Yogi Berra—One of the top catchers in baseball history who played on 10 world championship teams

No. 8 Bill Dickey—Also considered one of the top backstops of all time, hit .300 in 10 of his first 11 seasons

No. 9 Roger Maris—Two-time Most Valuable Player was best known for 61 home runs in 1961

No. 10 Phil Rizzuto—Won an American League Most Valuable Player award and a World Series MVP while playing for the Yankees' five-time world championship club from 1949 to 1953

No. 15 Thurman Munson—Former MVP and Gold Glove winner was known as a great clutch hitter who led the Yanks to two titles in 1977 and 1978

No. 16 Whitey Ford—One of the greatest Yankees pitchers of all time who still holds numerous World Series pitching records

No. 23 Don Mattingly—The nine-time Gold Glove winner tied the major league mark by hitting a home run in eight consecutive games and the most grand slams in one season with six in 1987

No. 32 Elston Howard—The first black player in Yankees history who won the American League's MVP award in 1963 and a World Series MVP award in 1958

No. 37 Casey Stengel—Greatest manager in Yankees history; won 10 pennants and 7 world championships in a 12-year span

No. 44 Reggie Jackson—Helped Yanks to two world championships including a once-in-a-lifetime performance of three home runs in one Series game in 1977

No. 49 Ron Guidry—Greatest single-season pitching performance in Yankees history with a 25–3 record that included the Yankees single-game strikeout mark of 18 in 1978

TRIVIA

In April 2000, two Yankees switch-hit home runs from both sides of the plate in the same game becoming the only duo to do so in major league history. Who were those two switch-hitters?

Answers to the trivia questions are on pages 186–187.

Department. The idea for the famous ornament originated in 1877 with a suggestion that it be placed on a medal to be given to Officer John McDowell, who was the first New York City policeman to be shot in the line of duty. In 1909 the famous insignia made its debut on the Highlanders uniforms by appearing in two places: the cap, of course, and the jersey's left sleeve.

Before 1909 the Highlanders wore a jersey that had the *N* on the right breast and a *Y* on the left, with one exception. During the 1905 season, the *N* and the *Y* were worn side by side in a monogram that resembles the legendary emblem that the modern-day Yankees wear.

Some people that you may recognize donned the New York Highlanders uniform, including a man who would go down in baseball history as the one who broke the color barrier when he signed Hall of Famer Jackie Robinson to play second base for the Brooklyn Dodgers. Wesley Branch Rickey was a 25-year-old part-time catcher for the Highlanders who appeared in 52 games, but one game in particular stands out.

It was June 28, 1907. The Highlanders hosted the Washington Senators, and Rickey got the nod behind the plate. Washington ran wild, stealing a record 13 bases in the game; however, the blame may not lie totally with Rickey.

Right-handed pitcher Lew Brockett, who replaced Earl Moore after one inning, pitched the final eight innings by allowing 22 base runners (14 hits, eight walks). Reportedly, Brockett did not pitch from the stretch, even with runners on, so the Senators had carte blanche to take shots at stealing bases. If that's true, then Rickey became the scapegoat.

The Washington Post ran the game story the morning after. "The Washingtons went on a base-running spree, waxed merry over a jag of pilfered sacks," was how it was written. "Rickey threw so poorly to bases that all a man had to put through a steal was to start. The

Washingtons soon discovered that as a thrower Rickey was many chips shy, and they paused in their travels merely long enough to get breath."

The Highlanders were sold to Colonels Tillinghast L'Hommedieu Huston and Jacob Ruppert for a sum of $460,000 following the 1912 season. The team nearly became known as the Knickerbockers because the new ownership wanted to use the club to promote Ruppert's beer business. Fans and media were up in arms, so the owners changed their minds and in April 1913, the New York Highlanders became the New York Yankees.

On April 10, 1913, the New York Yankees played the Washington Senators in D.C. in their first game, which they lost 2–1.

The rest is history.

Dugout Generals

Over the years, the task of managing the New York Yankees has been referred to as the toughest job in sports. In the history of the Yankees, there have been 31 different managers. Eight of the 31 have won a World Series as Yankees manager, but four of the eight make up the elite class of Yankees skippers, as they have combined for 21 of the Series titles.

Miller Huggins

He stood only 5'6" tall, but he once took on the almighty Babe Ruth. His name was Miller Huggins, and he's widely credited with being the first in a long line of great Yankees managers.

Huggins was a top-notch second baseman during his playing career. After being picked up by the Cardinals in 1910, he eventually became their manager in 1913. Huggins resigned from the Cardinals job and then began a 12-year managerial stint with the Yankees.

Yankees owner Jacob Ruppert had always admired Huggins from afar, so he wasn't going to let an opportunity get by without trying to secure the Hall of Fame manager.

Huggins guided the Yankees to their first American League championships in 1921 and 1922. Both times, they lost the World Series to the crosstown rival New York Giants. Finally, in 1923, the Yankees captured the first of their 26 world championships with a 4–2 World Series payback victory over, appropriately enough, the Giants.

During the 1925 season, Huggins made the most famous substitution in baseball history. It was June 1, 1925, when Huggins pinch-hit a 21-year-old rookie first baseman named Lou Gehrig for light-hitting shortstop Pee Wee Wanninger.

TOP 10

Triples

Player	Number of Triples
1. Lou Gehrig	183
2. Earle Combs	154
3. Joe DiMaggio	131
4. Wally Pipp	121
5. Tory Lazzeri	115
6. Babe Ruth	106
7. Bob Meusel	87
8. Tommy Henrich	73
9. Mickey Mantle	72
10. Bill Dickey	72

The 1926 Yankees climbed back on top, going from a seventh-place finish in 1925 to win the American League by three games to face the NL champion St. Louis Cardinals. The Redbirds won the series with a 3–2 victory in Game 7 at Yankee Stadium, but how the game ended is what's memorable about that World Series.

With the Yankees down to their final out, Babe Ruth walked for the fourth time in the game. Bob Meusel was at the plate (Meusel batted ahead of Gehrig) and Ruth, inexplicably, tried to steal second but was caught stealing by Cardinals catcher Bob O'Farrell, thus ending the game and the Series.

A tough loss for Huggins and the Yankees, but it became easier to accept the next season when the 1927 Yankees put together one of the greatest single seasons in baseball history. Their lineup was nicknamed "Murderers' Row" because it contained a relentless list of all-time great hitters, including four Hall of Famers.

Consider that Huggins had Earle Combs leading off, followed by Mark Koenig, Babe Ruth, Lou Gehrig, Bob Meusel, and Tony Lazzeri. Third baseman Joe Dugan hit seventh followed by the starting catcher, Pat Collins. And, of course, the pitcher batted ninth.

The team finished 110–44, 19 games ahead of the second-place Philadelphia A's and 59 games ahead of the last-place Boston Red

Sox. With a four-game sweep of the Pittsburgh Pirates in the World Series, Huggins had his second championship.

The Yanks would repeat in 1928. That year marked the final championship for Huggins in his tenure as Yankees skipper. Huggins suddenly died from blood poisoning in September 1929, and he was replaced by Art Fletcher for the remainder of the season. In 1932, the Yankees decided to honor their diminutive manager with the dedication of the first monument that was placed (in play) in center field. Huggins was inducted into the Hall of Fame in 1964.

Joe McCarthy

The Yankees were still reeling from the death of Miller Huggins less than two years earlier while looking for a return to the top following a third-place finish in 1930.

The winningest manager in New York Yankees history would begin his tenure with the 1931 season. Joe McCarthy was already a winning manager, with the 1929 National League champion Chicago Cubs, which made him even more attractive to Yankees brass.

Manager Joe McCarthy gets behind the camera to film Joe DiMaggio's swing during spring training before the 1939 season.

Even with a pennant to his credit, McCarthy was fired as Cubs manager following a second-place finish in 1930. The Yankees took notice of McCarthy's work in the senior circuit, so they grabbed the 44-year-old skipper. He took the team to a second-place finish with a 94–59 record, which was still a distant 13.5 games behind the first-place Philadelphia A's.

In 1932 McCarthy's Yanks won the pennant by 13 games with an incredible 107–47 mark (.695 winning percentage) and then took on "Mac's" old team, the Chicago Cubs, in the World Series.

The Yankees led the Series 2–0 when the scene shifted to Chicago. It was McCarthy's first game at Wrigley Field since he was unceremoniously let go by the Cubs a year after he won the pennant. Additionally, Babe Ruth and a number of other Yankees lambasted the Cubs for voting Mark Koenig a half share of the World Series pot. Koenig was an integral part of the Yankees championship teams in 1926, 1927, and 1928, and his former teammates felt he was getting a raw deal from the Cubs after he was acquired in a late-season trade.

The Yankees led 4–3 going into the fifth when it was time for a legendary baseball moment. With one out in the top of the fifth, Ruth came up against Cubs starter Charlie Root, whom he had homered off of in the first. On the first pitch, Ruth took a called strike. Root missed the strike zone with the next two but got another called strike to make the count 2–2. The crowd at Wrigley was on Ruth, not only for degrading the Cubs for how they treated Koenig, but in the previous inning the Babe had missed an attempt at a shoestring catch. Ruth then gestured toward center field and hit the next pitch to that spot over the wall, near the flagpole. To this day, no one really knows what Ruth was doing with his gesture. Did he point to the exact spot where he thought he would hit it? Or did he simply indicate to the Cubs bench and their fans, who were razzing the best player in an opposing uniform, that he still had one strike left? No matter, because the reality is Ruth hit that home run and the Yankees went on to win the Series in four straight, giving McCarthy his first world championship as a manager.

After three consecutive second-place finishes, McCarthy guided the club to four consecutive world championships from 1936 to 1939.

TRIVIA

There is only one former Yankees number one draft choice who has made it to the Hall of Fame. Can you name him?

Answers to the trivia questions are on pages 186–187.

In 1940 McCarthy's Yanks were involved in their first real pennant race. During his winning years, McCarthy's teams were never really threatened because they had such big leads while coasting to the pennant. But in 1940 the Yankees and two other clubs—the Detroit Tigers and the Cleveland Indians—were locked up in a bid for the American League championship.

In September the Yankees would win nine of 10 to pull within two and a half games of first-place Detroit with three days left. But they lost to Philadelphia, and the Tigers clinched the pennant with a win over Cleveland.

Another run of three straight pennants led to two more World Series championships and a Yankees record total of seven in all for McCarthy, who became the all-time winningest manager in franchise history during the 1941 season, when he surpassed Miller Huggins's total of 1,067 victories.

McCarthy's final two full seasons in 1944 and 1945 were both disappointing as the Yanks finished third and fourth respectively.

When off-the-field events began to undermine McCarthy's authority early in the 1946 season, the writing was on the wall. On May 24, McCarthy was fired as Yankees manager and was replaced by Bill Dickey.

In 1957 McCarthy was voted into baseball's Hall of Fame, and in 1976 he was added to Monument Park with a plaque in his honor. McCarthy died in January 1978 at the age of 90.

Casey Stengel

With 10 American League pennants and seven World Series championships in a 12-year span defining his résumé, Charles Dillon Stengel has to go down as the greatest manager in the history of the New York Yankees.

Stengel was not only a great Yankees manager, but he was also a former major league player and one of the greatest quote machines to ever put on a uniform. Beginning in 1912, when he debuted as an outfielder with the Brooklyn Superbas (the team that came to be known as the Dodgers), Casey Stengel made the major leagues his life until he retired in 1965 after breaking his hip in a fall at Shea Stadium. Stengel's 14-year playing career included three World Series appearances. In 1916 Stengel's Brooklyn Robins lost to the American League champion Boston Red Sox. Casey returned to the Series with the New York Giants in 1922 and tasted the thrill of victory in five games over none other than the New York Yankees.

Casey's colorful legacy extends all the way back to his minor league career. While playing in a Southern League game at Montgomery, Stengel reportedly lowered himself into a manhole in the outfield to fool the hitter into thinking no one was at the position. When a fly ball was hit in his direction, Stengel came out of the hole to make the catch.

Casey's gift of gab was priceless. "Stengel-ese," as it came to be known, was a real treat for the beat writers who were assigned to cover the colorful skipper during his managerial career. Oratorical gems, like, "There comes a time in every man's life, and I've had plenty of them" or "Managing is getting paid for home runs someone else hits," became part of Stengel's legend.

Stengel's managerial career began in the same place as his playing career, when he was named pilot of the Brooklyn Dodgers in 1934. Three sub-.500 seasons in Flatbush led to being fired. Stengel signed on for a six-year stint in Boston where he managed the Braves and failed to finish higher than fifth in the standings. After being dismissed by the Braves in the spring of 1944, Stengel began a five-year tenure managing in the minors.

In 1946 Casey took over the Oakland Oaks of the Pacific Coast League, and after a steady, upward climb, he piloted the team to a first-place finish in 1948. That fact was not lost on Yankees general manager George Weiss—the Oaks general manager in 1946—who hired Stengel on October 12, 1948, to manage the Yankees beginning with the 1949 season.

The move was ridiculed throughout baseball. After all, Stengel had been a losing manager at two previous stops, how would he get this Yankees team back on top? Little did the cynics know that Stengel's hiring would begin a run that saw the Yankees win five consecutive World Series, not to mention 14 American League pennants, in the next 16 years. Unlike his previous managerial stints, Stengel was handed a talented roster that featured the likes of Joe DiMaggio, Yogi Berra, and Phil Rizzuto. Casey had good pitching as well with Eddie Lopat, Allie Reynolds, Vic Raschi, and Tommy Byrne forming an excellent starting staff.

Nineteen forty-nine provided a lot of excitement, not just because the Yankees were contending for the pennant, but because of whom they were contending with—their hated rivals, the Boston Red Sox. With eight games remaining in the season, the Yankees went into Boston on September 24 with a two-game lead but proceeded to get swept and trail the Bosox by one with five left. The Yankees remained a game behind heading into the final two-game series of the season against Boston at Yankee Stadium. Stengel's Yanks needed a sweep to win the pennant.

The Yankees tied the Red Sox for first with a 5–4 victory in the opening game of the Series, so it was a do-or-die season finale for all the marbles. Right-hander Vic Raschi started for the Yankees against Red Sox righty Ellis Kinder, who was 23–5 going into the final game. The Yanks maintained a 1–0 lead going into the eighth, but Stengel's crew opened up a 5–1 lead against a fatigued Mel Parnell, who came in relief after having pitched in the previous day's game. The Yanks went on to win 5–3, and Stengel captured the first of his 10 American League pennants.

A five-game victory in the 1949 Series against none other than the Brooklyn Dodgers silenced the critics. Under Casey, the Yankees went on a record-setting run of five consecutive World Series championships that lasted through the 1953 season.

During this great run, the Yankees were going through a historical transition. Joe DiMaggio was nearing the end of his career while the Yankees were confident that a 19-year-old phenom named Mickey Mantle was going to carry the baton to keep the team on top.

Stengel's relationship with Mantle was almost of a parental nature. Casey not only patted Mickey on the back to encourage the youngster, but he would scold and punish him as well to teach him how to play the game the right way. Stengel's influence on Mantle would help shape the destiny of his Yankees. The team didn't skip a beat, even with DiMaggio's retirement after the 1951 season.

By the NUMBERS

Date Team Was Purchased	Owner
January 9, 1903	Frank Farrell and Bill Devery
January 11, 1915	Col. Jacob Ruppert and Col. Tillinghast L'Hommedieu Huston
May 21, 1922	Col. Ruppert buys out Col. Huston for $1,500,000
January 25, 1945	Dan Topping, Del Webb, and Larry MacPhail buy team from Ruppert estate
November 2, 1964	CBS Corp.
January 3, 1973	George M. Steinbrenner

It appeared that no one was going to be able to stop Casey's Yanks, but in 1954, someone did. For the first time in his Yankees managerial career, Stengel would not go to the World Series. They didn't go down without a fight, though. The 1954 Yankees won 103 games yet finished eight games back of the pennant-winning Cleveland Indians, who won a record-setting 111 contests.

Nineteen fifty-five saw a return to the top for the Yankees, but Stengel experienced World Series defeat for the first time as a manager. Brooklyn took the Series in seven games.

In 1956, it was the same two rivals again, but a perfect game thrown by the Yanks' Don Larsen in Game 5 overshadowed another championship for Stengel, his sixth, in a thrilling seven-game showdown.

Stengel won his eighth pennant in 1957, but this time it was the Yankees and the Milwaukee Braves who battled in the Series. The Braves, led by Hall of Famers Hank Aaron, Warren Spahn, and Eddie Mathews, defeated the Yanks in seven games, but the teams rematched in 1958, and the Bombers rallied from a three-games-to-one deficit to give Stengel his seventh and final World Series championship as Yankees manager.

The only other time that Stengel finished out of first place during his tenure was in 1959 when the Yankees came in third, 15 games behind the American League champion Chicago White Sox. Unfortunately, at that point, Stengel's bosses were beginning to wonder if he was starting to lose his touch.

While the Pittsburgh Pirates were in the process of pulling off one of the biggest upsets in World Series history against the heavily favored Yankees in 1960, front-office types were planning to hand Stengel his walking papers. They did so just five days after Bill Mazeroski's Series-winning home run cleared the left-field wall at Forbes Field. At 70 years old, Stengel was let go by the Yankees. The club cited health reasons, but it was suspected that the Yankees were simply not happy with Stengel's performance in the dugout anymore.

The "Old Professor" went on to become the first manager in the history of the New York Mets in 1962 where he piloted a perennial loser until 1965 when health reasons did force him into retirement.

As a Yankees manager, Stengel holds the club record with 1,149 wins and a .623 winning percentage, not to mention his postseason accomplishments. Stengel made lots of enemies among his players, but there were many supporters as well. Former Yankees second baseman Jerry Coleman, at a Yankees Old-Timers Day, called Stengel "brilliant." "Many people thought he was a clown, but Casey knew what he was doing," said Coleman, who played for the "Old Professor" for nine seasons. "We won because of him in most cases."

Former pitcher Bob Turley, who helped Stengel win his seventh and final World Series in 1958, said, "Casey was interesting and very talkative," while former first baseman Bill "Moose" Skowron credited Stengel with getting him into the big leagues in 1954. "He gave me an opportunity," Skowron said.

Stengel was inducted into the Hall of Fame in 1966 and had his No. 37 retired by the Yankees in 1970. In 1976 Stengel joined McCarthy with a plaque on the wall of Monument Park.

Joe Torre

The Yankees had just come off of a crushing five-game loss to Seattle in the 1995 divisional series, and the team was in flux. Buck Showalter was let go as Yankees manager, and the search was on. Yankees senior vice president of media relations, Arthur Richman, suggested Joe Torre to Yankees owner George Steinbrenner.

On November 2, 1995, "Clueless Joe" was front-page news in the local papers as Joseph Paul Torre became the 31ˢᵗ manager in franchise history. Torre's entry into Yankees lore mirrored that of Casey Stengel. Like Casey, Torre had managed in the big leagues before getting the Yankees job and had been unsuccessful, posting an 894–1,003 mark in three previous managerial stints. Like Stengel, Torre was given a roster full of talent, more than he ever had at his disposal before.

TRIVIA

What was Derek Jeter's first uniform number when he made his major league debut in 1995?

a) 70
b) 67
c) 55
d) 2

Answers to the trivia questions are on pages 186–187.

Unlike Stengel, Torre was better on the field during his playing days. Torre compiled an outstanding 18-year playing career for the Milwaukee/Atlanta Braves, St. Louis Cardinals, and New York Mets. In 1971 the former Gold Glove–winning catcher was at third for the Cardinals, beginning that season with a 22-game hitting streak. He never looked back. Six months later, Torre locked up the National League's Most Valuable Player award with a league-leading .363 average, 24 home runs, and a league-leading 137 RBIs.

On May 31, 1977, Torre accepted the job as a player and manager of the Mets. Torre retired as a player later that year, but he managed the Mets through the 1981 split season and then took over the helm of his former team, the Atlanta Braves, in 1982. Under Torre, the Braves came flying out of the gate with a 13–0 start, and they held on for the division title in the National League West. It would be the Brooklyn-born manager's only first-place finish until he became a Yankees skipper. Torre was let go as Atlanta's manager following the 1984 season and spent the next few years as a broadcaster for the Anaheim Angels.

The former Cardinal returned to roost when he was hired to manage the Redbirds in August 1990, replacing Whitey Herzog, who decided to step down. Torre lasted until June 1995, and a little more than a year later he was headed to the World Series.

Incredibly, during 40-plus years spent in the service of major league baseball, Joe Torre, who grew up on the streets of New York

By the NUMBERS

31—Number of men who have managed the Yankees (in alphabetical order)

Manager	Year	Won	Lost
Yogi Berra	1964, 1984–85	192	148
Frank Chance	1913–14	117	168
Hal Chase	1910–11	85	78
Bucky Dent	1989–90	36	53
Bill Dickey	1946	57	48
Bill Donovan	1915–17	220	239
Kid Elberfeld	1908	27	71
Art Fletcher	1929	6	5
Dallas Green	1989	56	65
Clark Griffith	1903–08	419	370
Bucky Harris	1947–48	191	117
Ralph Houk	1961–63, 1966–73	944	806
Dick Howser	1980	103	59
Miller Huggins	1918–29	1067	719
Johnny Keane	1965–66	81	101
Clyde King	1982	29	33
Bob Lemon	1978–79, 1981–82	99	73
Billy Martin	1975–78, 1979, 1983, 1985, 1988	556	385
Joe McCarthy	1931–46	1,460	867
Stump Merrill	1990–91	120	155
Gene Michael	1981–82	92	76
Johnny Neun	1946	8	6
Roger Peckinpaugh	1914	10	10
Lou Piniella	1986–87, 1988	224	193
Bob Shawkey	1930	86	68
Buck Showalter	1992–95	313	268
George Stallings	1909–10	153	138
Casey Stengel	1949–60	1,079	699
Joe Torre	1996–Present	982	634
Bill Virdon	1974–75	142	124
Harry Wolverton	1912	50	102

City, had absolutely nothing to do with the Yankees in any capacity. But in a relatively short time, he became one of the most significant figures to ever don the Yankees pinstripes.

Torre's first game as Yankees manager was a 7–1 win at Cleveland. It also marked the debut of rookie Derek Jeter as the Yankees starting shortstop. The Yankees were making a strong run for the American League East crown as they hit September. The magical season took its next turn as the Bombers clinched the East on September 25.

An opening-game loss to Texas in the divisional playoffs was merely a blip on the radar screen, as Torre's Yankees stormed back to win three in a row and move on to the skipper's first American League championship series as the pinstriped general.

The Yankees won their 34th American League pennant in a five-game victory, and Torre was headed to the World Series for the first time in his career. "It was like finally tasting that hot fudge sundae that you've always craved," said the victorious manager in the winning locker room afterward. "It tastes especially sweet right now."

The 1996 Series against the Atlanta Braves was the opening act of Torre's storybook run as Yankees skipper. The Bombers lost Game 1 and Game 2 at Yankee Stadium, both by blowouts. Things looked bleak for a 23rd World Series win. But Torre proved to be prophetic when he assured Yankees owner George Steinbrenner that the Yankees would come back and win the Series. In fact, Torre told the nervous owner that the club would go down to Atlanta for Game 3, 4, and 5, and they would sweep the next three on the road. Sure enough, the Yankees won Game 3, and then Game 4 became the turning point of the Series. The Braves built a 6–0 lead just five innings into the game, but the Yankees rallied and tied the game at six on Jim Leyritz's three-run homer in the eighth. The Yankees scored a run in the tenth to pull out a 7–6 win to even the Series at two games apiece.

In Game 5 Andy Pettitte was brilliant and Torre stayed with him into the ninth. The Yankees held on for a 1–0 win and a chance to wrap up the World Series at Yankee Stadium two nights later. Unfortunately, personal issues clouded Torre's impending moment of triumph. His brother, Frank, was having an issue with his heart and needed surgery. Successful surgery was performed and on the eve of his greatest accomplishment in baseball, Joe Torre greeted his brother Frank in the hospital as he recovered.

On Saturday night, October 26, a packed house at Yankee Stadium awaited the chance to coronate the newest Yankees championship team.

Torre gave the ball to left-hander Jimmy Key, and he did not disappoint as he went six strong innings. Catcher Joe Girardi hit a key triple off of losing pitcher Greg Maddux. When Yankees third baseman Charlie Hayes caught the final out on a foul pop from the Braves Mark Lemke, the stadium exploded with joy.

The emotional scene inside the dugout was one to remember. Joseph Paul Torre joined the ranks of Miller Huggins, Joe McCarthy, and Casey Stengel. He was a championship-winning Yankees manager. "I'd been close several times," said the Yankees skipper. "It always fell on the wrong side of the fence."

Torre's reputation is one of being a player's manager, but when needed, the Brooklyn-born skipper can be very tough. Being able to motivate was never a problem. The Yankees made the playoffs in 1997 but failed to advance past the first round. The five-game loss to Cleveland hurt so much that the team vowed to make 1998 their year. No one realized how far the Yankees would carry that vow, but in 1998, Joe Torre's New York Yankees blew through the American League by winning a record 114 games. The club went on to win 11 of 13 in the postseason capped off by a four-game sweep of the National League champion San Diego Padres.

Two more championships would follow to make it three in a row and four overall. In just a five-year span, Joe Torre had already won more titles than Huggins and trailed just Stengel and McCarthy on the all-time Yankees list. Torre put the winning in perspective, "It seemed like we had been here [with the Yankees] forever, but it's still brand-new because you always have to constantly prove yourself."

Torre's Yankees would go on to make the playoffs in his first 11 years, the first pinstriped skipper to accomplish such a feat, and his 75 postseason victories leads all managers. When it's all said and done, a place in Monument Park and the baseball Hall of Fame awaits New York's native son, not to mention a taste of that special hot fudge sundae.

Other Winning Managers

Of the remaining five titles, Ralph Houk won twice, while Bucky Harris, Billy Martin, and Bob Lemon each won one apiece.

It was ironic that Houk took over for the fired Stengel in 1961, and the Yankees went off to one of their greatest seasons under the man known as a player's manager. Houk's 1962 team repeated as champions but not without some drama in the seventh game of the World Series in San Francisco.

The Yankees clung to a 1–0 lead in the bottom of the ninth. With two outs, the Giants had runners at second and third with Willie McCovey due up against Ralph Terry, who had tossed a brilliant game to that point. Conventional wisdom would dictate walking McCovey, but Houk made one of the most pivotal decisions of his managerial career by pitching to, and getting McCovey to line out to, Bobby Richardson at second for the final out.

If McCovey would've gotten a hit, Houk would've been subjected to some of the most vicious second guessing ever showered upon a big-league skipper. The Major piloted the Yankees until 1964. He returned for a second tenure as Yankees skipper from 1966 through the 1973 season, at which point he resigned.

Harris ran the team for two seasons, capturing the 1947 World Series in a seven-game thriller over Brooklyn. Harris was known as a player's manager. His nickname was "the Boy Wonder" after he won a World Series as a player/manager for the Washington Senators in 1924.

Billy Martin was the most tenured and enigmatic manager to ever run the Yankees. Martin took over the team on August 1, 1975, replacing Bill Virdon, who one year earlier had taken the Yankees to a near-first-place finish in the division. Martin's first full season produced the Yanks first pennant since 1964 and a year later the first World Series championship since 1962. In mid-1978, Martin resigned amid controversy but was rehired to take the team again in

1979. Billy the Kid was let go after 1979 but returned as manager for a third time in 1983. His third dismissal came after the 1983 season. Martin later came back for the 1985 season and a part of the 1988 season. The fiery Yankees skipper tragically perished in an automobile accident on Christmas night in 1989.

Bob Lemon had two tenures, but the first one was the most famous. Lemon replaced Martin in July 1978. The Yankees were reeling and grew weary of Martin's tough-guy tactics. Lemon was more laid-back, and it was just what the 1978 team needed as they went on to the greatest comeback in franchise history and a second consecutive World Series championship.

Martin and Lemon flip-flopped again in 1979, and then the former pitcher returned for the second half of the 1981 season and led the Yanks to the Series only to lose to the Dodgers in six games. Lemon began the 1982 season but was replaced by Gene Michael.

Two other managers took the Yankees to postseason play, but not a World Series berth. Dick Howser led the Yanks to 103 victories and a fourth AL East crown, but they were swept by the Kansas City Royals in the ALCS. After the loss, Howser was let go.

The other such manager, Buck Showalter, had postseason play in the form of the first American League wild-card berth. Showalter took over the team in 1992 and finished 10 games under .500, but the next season the team improved from 76 wins to 88 and a second-place finish in the East. Showalter had instilled a new attitude in the Yankees who needed a makeover after a disastrous start to the 1990s. In 1994 the Yankees were leading the East and the American League when a labor dispute ended the season and cancelled the World Series. When the teams returned to play in 1995, the landscape of major league baseball had changed with the addition of a wild-card team and a change in the playoff format.

Under Showalter, the Yankees stumbled for most of the 1995 season, but they put on a surge in the

TRIVIA

Who was the last Yankees pitcher to hit a home run?

Answers to the trivia questions are on pages 186–187.

final month winning 20 of their final 25 games, including 11 of 12 in the final two weeks to secure their first postseason berth of any kind in 14 years.

Showalter's Yanks would lose a tough five-game divisional series to Seattle. He was dismissed following that loss.

Despite the fact that Joe Torre took over the team in 1996 and went on a run of four championships in five years, it could be argued that Showalter's fingerprints were all over that Yankees run.

Yankees great Yogi Berra was the only other pennant-winning manager in the team's history as he won the 1964 flag but lost a seven-game series to the St. Louis Cardinals. Berra was fired and replaced by the former Cardinals manager Johnny Keane, who had just beaten the Yanks in the Series. Yogi was brought back as Yankees skipper for the 1984 season and lasted until 16 games into the 1985 campaign, when he was let go.

Other people, such as Gene Michael, Lou Piniella, Dallas Green, and Bucky Dent, have managed the Yankees at one time or another. Whoever replaces Torre as Yankees manager will have an awful lot of legacy to live up to.

In 1934 Yankees Lost More Than Pennant Race

The 1934 Yankees were extremely confident they would return to the top of the American League. Two years prior, the Yankees won their fourth world championship, but in 1933 the Bombers dropped off to a second-place finish, seven games behind the American League champion Washington Senators.

Nineteen thirty-four would be their year again, or at least they thought so. The Yankees featured seven Hall of Famers on their roster (including manager Joe McCarthy) and figured to be the odds-on favorite. They did not count on a big-time challenge from the Detroit Tigers.

The Tigers had four Hall of Famers of their own and featured a hard-hitting lineup that included second baseman Charlie Gehringer and first baseman Hank Greenberg.

Both teams got off to slow starts. On June 1, the Yankees were 22–17 while the Tigers were 22–18, but they were 2–3 in the American League. Surprisingly, the Cleveland Indians were sitting on top. New York was second, one game back, while Detroit was in third place, two games back (but four in the loss column).

Just about midway through the season, the Yankees received a major scare. It was June 29. The Yankees were playing an exhibition game at Norfolk, Virginia and Lou Gehrig was in the lineup. The "Iron Man" was hit in the head by a pitched ball, which could've ended his historic consecutive-games streak right then and there. Gehrig recovered enough to play the next day in a game at Washington where he stroked three triples in his first three at-bats. However, the game was called after four and a half innings with the

Yanks leading 4–1. Because the Senators did not complete their fifth at-bat, the game was called off to be replayed in its entirety.

June turned into July, and the Yankees led Detroit by one game, two in the loss column. On August 1, following their 10–7 win over Cleveland and a 7–4 Yankees loss to Boston, the Tigers moved ahead of New York into first place for good.

The season took a historic turn on August 10, when Babe Ruth told the Associated Press that he planned to retire as an active player at the end of the season. "I really don't know what the future holds for me," said Ruth. "I would like to remain in the game as a manager and perhaps do a little pinch hitting on Saturdays and Sundays or days I figure it could help the gate."

Babe Ruth towels off after his final game as a Yankee on September 30, 1934.

By the NUMBERS

10—Number of Yankees who have hit for the cycle

Player	Year(s)
Bert Daniels	1912
Bob Meusel (3)	1921, 1922, 1928
Tony Lazzeri	1932
Lou Gehrig (2)	1934, 1937
Joe DiMaggio (2)	1937, 1948
Buddy Rosar	1940
Joe Gordon	1940
Mickey Mantle	1957
Bobby Murcer	1972
Tony Fernandez	1995

On August 14 the rivals began a five-game series with a double-header at Yankee Stadium. Before a record crowd of 77,000, the Tigers swept the twin bill, 9–5 and 7–3, ending up six and a half games up on the Bombers.

As the teams hit September, Detroit led the American League with an 83–43 mark. The Yankees were second at 79–48, four and a half games behind with 25 to play.

The two leaders were scheduled for a four-game showdown beginning on September 17 in Detroit. With 15 games to play before the head-to-head clash, the Yankees needed to put themselves in position to make those games count. It did not happen. New York went 8–7 while the Tigers went 9–6 leading up to the first game of the showdown. The Yanks trailed by five and a half as they opened the key series in Motown.

In Game 1, Detroit was smug. They did not use their best pitcher, Preacher Rowe, against the Yankees' ace, Lefty Gomez. Tigers player/manager Mickey Cochrane elected to start Alvin Crowder, and it paid off as he beat Gomez with a six-hit shutout and a 3–0 Tigers win. The victory left the Yankees six and a half games back.

A rumor surfaced of a plot to kidnap Detroit's ace pitcher. The Tigers denied any knowledge of this story or that extra police protection was provided because of it. There were extra police assigned to the team, but that was because of the frenzy that was starting to develop among the Tigers fans in Detroit.

Game 2 was a repeat of Game 1, but this time Rowe blanked the Yankees on seven hits in a 2–0 win. It was seven and half back and counting for New York.

The Yankees got some payback in Game 3 with a 5–2 win and then closed the series on Thursday, September 20, with an 11–7 win. The split left the Yankees five and a half back with eight to play.

The Yankees officially eliminated themselves on September 24. With Detroit idle, the Bombers were shut out by Boston at Yankee Stadium, 5–0.

Ruth made his final appearance as a Yankee on September 30 in Washington. He was 0 for 3 in his pinstripe finale.

Some notable numbers and facts from that 1934 campaign: Lou Gehrig won the batting crown with a .363 average. The Tigers' Charlie Gehringer was second at .356. Gehrig also hit 30 home runs at Yankee Stadium, a team mark that was met by Roger Maris in 1961.

Tigers manager Mickey Cochrane won the American League MVP award in 1934. Ironically, a little two-year-old boy who was named after Cochrane would grow up to become one of the greatest Yankees who ever put on the pinstripes. His name was Mickey Mantle.

Finally, in November 1934, the Yankees purchased the contract of Joe DiMaggio from the San Francisco Seals.

IF ONLY . . . Babe Ruth really did call his shot against the Cubs in the 1932 World Series. According to eyewitness accounts, Ruth was signaling to the crowd what the count was after each pitch he saw from the Cubs' Charlie Root. After putting up two fingers to indicate the count was 2–2, the Bambino launched a tremendous blast that traveled past the flagpole in centerfield. Ruth later claimed that he did point toward center field and that he told the Cubs bench that he would hit the next pitch right to the spot at which he had just pointed.

Joe DiMaggio: 56 More Than Just an Unbeatable Number

The greatest tribute ever paid to Joe DiMaggio's incredible 56-game hitting streak in 1941 was that many baseball historians labeled it as a record that would never be broken.

That mantra has stood the test of time with very few to have even approached the magic number for hitting in consecutive games. Pete Rose came the closest so far by hitting in 44 consecutive games in 1978.

The Yankee Clipper's streak began on May 15 at Yankee Stadium against the Chicago White Sox. Consider that DiMaggio started his historic run with a single off an overweight left-hander named Edgar Smith. This is pertinent because of who starts the game when the streak ends in July.

In Game 2 DiMaggio got two hits, including a 420-foot home run to the left-center-field bleachers as the Yanks rallied in the ninth to beat the Chisox.

The streak continued right into June and on June 17, the Yankee Clipper reached the first significant milestone of his hot stretch, but not without some good fortune. DiMaggio's only hit of the game came in the seventh inning of an 8–7 defeat (White Sox). Joltin' Joe hit a sharp grounder to Sox shortstop Luke Appling, but the ball took a bad hop and hit Appling in the shoulder to give DiMaggio a 30-game hitting streak, a new Yankees franchise record. The mark was formerly held by Roger Peckinpaugh and Earle Combs.

After the game, DiMaggio went to the Polo Grounds to watch heavyweight champion Joe Louis defend his title with a 13th-round knockout.

Joe DiMaggio lines a single to left to keep his incredible hitting streak alive at 42 straight games on June 29, 1941.

On June 29 against Washington, DiMaggio hit in his 42nd straight game to break George Sisler's modern-day standard. July 1 saw DiMaggio tie the Baltimore Orioles' Wee Willie Keeler's 1897 mark of hitting in 44 consecutive games, and then he went for the record the next day against the Red Sox. DiMaggio set the new record in style with a three-run homer that helped beat Boston. The numbers that the Yankee Clipper put up during this memorable run are remarkable.

In the 45-game streak, DiMaggio had 67 hits, including 12 doubles and 13 home runs, as well as hitting at a .374 clip.

By the NUMBERS

8—Number of Yankees who have won the AL Rookie of the Year award

Name	Position	Year
Gil McDougald	infielder	1951
Bob Grim	pitcher	1954
Tony Kubek	infielder	1957
Tom Tresh	infielder	1962
Stan Bahnsen	pitcher	1968
Thurman Munson	catcher	1970
Dave Righetti	pitcher	1981
Derek Jeter	shortstop	1996

Joltin' Joe had certainly had hot streaks before. In 1933, while playing for the San Francisco Seals of the Pacific Coast League, DiMaggio hit in 61 straight games and felt it should have continued. According to reports, in what would have been his 62nd consecutive game, DiMaggio hit a ball toward the hole between short and third. The shortstop fielded it and threw low to first where the first baseman could not scoop it for the out. The play was ruled an error, but DiMaggio felt it should have been a hit.

A four-hit game on July 11 powered the Yanks to a 6–2 win over the St. Louis Browns, their 11th in a row, and it stretched DiMaggio's incredible streak to 50 in a row.

The Yankees' winning streak reached 14 in a row after a double-header sweep of the White Sox. DiMaggio followed right along. He had three hits in the opener and a single in the nightcap to extend his streak to 53 straight.

Consecutive game 54 was one where DiMaggio once again was fortunate. In the sixth inning of a 7–1 loss to the White Sox that snapped the club's 14-game winning streak, DiMaggio hit a topper toward third that went for an infield hit. Was the streak ever going to end? That was the question on the minds of fans and media alike.

The next day DiMaggio saw his old friend Edgar Smith, the pitcher against whom he began the streak, and the Yankees Clipper extended the hitting streak to 55 in a row with a single and a double.

The Yankees opened a three-game series at Cleveland on Wednesday, July 16, and DiMaggio kept things going as he stroked three more hits to extend the streak to the magic number 56.

On July 17, history was made as more than 67,000 fans packed into Cleveland's Municipal Stadium to witness the end of Joe DiMaggio's record-setting 56-game hitting streak. The Indians starter that day was portly left-hander Al Smith. Remember, the streak began against an overweight southpaw named Edgar Smith.

DiMaggio had three official at-bats in the game, but two of those were foiled by Indians third baseman Ken Keltner, who made two outstanding defensive plays to rob Hall of Famer DiMaggio.

In the first inning, DiMaggio hit a shot toward the third base line, but Keltner made a backhanded stab and threw across the diamond for the out.

DiMaggio walked in the third. Again in the seventh, Keltner made a backhanded grab for a ball hit toward the line, and again he threw out the Yankee Clipper at first.

In the eighth, DiMaggio came to the plate with the bases loaded. The Indians switched pitchers, choosing to go with right-hander Jim Bagby in relief of Al Smith. With the count at 2–1, Bagby got DiMaggio to hit into a double play. The Yankees won the game 4–3, but the streak was over.

But 56 straight games with at least one base hit was an amazing accomplishment. During the run, DiMaggio amassed 91 hits, including 57 singles, 16 doubles, four triples, and 15 home runs for 161 total bases.

After the game, DiMaggio said, "The streak doesn't mean a thing. Naturally there was some strain even after breaking the record, but I'm free and easy now."

"That's the kind of pitch you either hit or don't hit," said Bagby afterward. "Fortunately, he hit it right for our side."

DiMaggio resumed hitting for another 16 straight games until August 3 when he went hitless in a doubleheader. Another DiMaggio streak ended that day as he failed to reach base.

Even in the streak-ending game against Cleveland, DiMaggio drew a walk, but for the first time in 84 games, Joltin' Joe failed to get aboard.

TRIVIA

Yankees great Mickey
Mantle was a 16-time
All-Star. How many of
those appearances were
as a first baseman?

Answers to the trivia questions are on pages 186–187.

On August 4 at Washington, DiMaggio snapped a 0-for-10 skid, which prompted *New York Times* reporter John Drebinger to write, "he smashed a single to left and the boys on the bench, from Manager Joe McCarthy down the line, exhaled a great sigh of relief." As the season went on, every time that DiMaggio didn't get a hit in a game was cause for alarm.

After going hitless for an entire three-game series against the Philadelphia Athletics, during a doubleheader at Detroit, DiMaggio suffered a sprained ankle that put him in the hospital.

In his first five seasons in pinstripes, the Yankee Clipper had failed to play in every game, which he wanted to amend for the 1941 campaign. The ankle injury kept him out for nearly three weeks, but DiMaggio returned to close out what would be an MVP season for Joltin' Joe. When it was all said and done, the numbers were quite impressive. A .357 batting average, keyed by 193 hits (84 for extra bases); the marquee numbers showed 30 home runs and a league-leading 125 runs batted in. The most amazing statistic of DiMaggio's year was a total of 13 strikeouts in 541 at-bats.

In November DiMaggio took home his second AL Most Valuable Player award. Despite Ted Williams hitting more than .400, the Yankee Clipper beat out the "Splendid Splinter" by 37 votes, and many felt that the 56-game hitting streak was what made the difference.

Lou Gehrig's Disease: Did Babe (not Ruth) See It Coming?

When you think of Lou Gehrig, you think of 2,130 consecutive games played, but you must also think of ALS. Amyotrophic Lateral Sclerosis is a neuromuscular disease that took the great career of the Iron Horse and then his life.

The disease causes rapid loss of control over muscles and usually death within three to five years. There are some who say that Gehrig may have played his last few seasons with the disease, but if you examine his numbers, you notice the sharp drop off when he began the 1939 season, which turned out to be his last.

Baseball historian and well-known broadcaster Keith Olbermann conducted an interview about the Yankees great with former first baseman Babe Dahlgren in 1989. Dahlgren was the player who succeeded Gehrig in 1939 when he elected to take himself out of the lineup. According to Dahlgren, there was an incident that occurred years earlier that may have been a portent of what was to come. In Dahlgren's rookie year (1935) he played first base for the Boston Red Sox against the Yankees in a game at Fenway Park. It was a wet afternoon, so after Gehrig dumped a single into short right field, he rounded first as he usually does, to make the outfielder throw it in quickly. At that point, Gehrig's spikes got caught in the muddy track, forcing him to the ground. Dahlgren told Olbermann that Gehrig had trouble getting up and that, to him, it looked like more than just a conventional injury. After hearing the story, one could speculate that Gehrig was already feeling the effects of the disease, even as early as 1935.

But not according to studies done since that time. Because baseball is a sport where performance is measured by certain standards

Yankees teammates Lou Gehrig (right) and Babe Dahlgren embrace during a game on May 2, 1939, the day Gehrig took himself out of the lineup to be replaced by Dahlgren, ending Gehrig's 14-season string of 2,130 consecutive games.

of achievement, the numbers that the Iron Horse put up during the 1938 season could have provided a "red flag" that something was physically wrong. It also could have meant that the natural progression of father time was beginning to catch up to the Iron Horse.

In May 1938 Gehrig got stuck in an 0-for-11 skid and was dropped to sixth in the batting order by manager Joe McCarthy. In July the Yankees slugger was rumored to be suffering with a fractured right thumb. Gehrig had played and performed through nagging injuries before, but now he couldn't totally overcome the handicap. For the first time since his first full season in 1925, Gehrig did not hit more than .300, instead settling for .295, the exact same batting average he had in that initial campaign. There were reports that Gehrig's superior fielding abilities at first base were beginning to drop off. Balls that Gehrig used to gobble up were easily getting past him now for base hits. During spring training in 1939, second baseman Joe Gordon began shading more toward first to help Gehrig out. At bat the Yankees great was a shell of his former self. He was hardly getting the ball out of the infield and was being thrown out at second on balls he used to coast into doubles.

His final big league game was April 30, 1939, against Washington. His batting average was an embarrassing .143, and he knew his time had come. Later that season, Gehrig actually played the final three innings of an exhibition game in Kansas City but could do nothing like he used to. At that point, the Columbia grad decided to find out what was wrong. After a week of tests at the Mayo Clinic in Rochester, Minnesota, he was diagnosed with the disease on June 21. After being honored with his day at Yankee Stadium on July 4, Gehrig began the process of battling the disease. Unconfirmed reports of cures began to trickle in.

There were also those who had no knowledge whatsoever of ALS, and they were making false accusations such as the one that appeared as an exclusive in one of the New York newspapers in mid-August 1940. The story blamed Gehrig's illness for the three-time defending champion Yankees' struggle to make it four in a row. The claim was that the team was being infected with the same disease, thus inhibiting their performance. Gehrig's teammates denied that they were feeling the ill effects of ALS or any other disease, and the Iron Horse threatened a lawsuit. The unnamed publication issued a public apology to Gehrig, saying a thorough investigation revealed that the disease was non-communicable. No further legal action was taken.

Earlier that year, the Yankees announced that Gehrig's No. 4 would be retired. No one else would ever wear that number on a Yankees uniform. It was the first time that a baseball team retired a player's number. For the Yankees it was the first of many.

Gehrig battled the disease until his death on June 2, 1941. The Yankees great died at 10:10 PM at his home on Delafield Avenue in the Riverdale section of the Bronx. The next day, Gehrig's body lay in state for public viewing at the Christ Protestant Episcopal Church in

TRIVIA

How many players have recorded their 3,000th career hit in a Yankees uniform?

Answers to the trivia questions are on pages 186–187.

TOP 10

All-Time Hit List

1.	Lou Gehrig	2,721
2.	Babe Ruth	2,518
3.	Mickey Mantle	2,415
4.	Bernie Williams	2,336
5.	Joe DiMaggio	2,214
6.	Don Mattingly	2,153
7.	Derek Jeter	2,150
8.	Yogi Berra	2,148
9.	Bill Dickey	1,969
10.	Earle Combs	1,866

Riverdale. For two hours, from 8:00 PM to 10:00 PM, a reported crowd of 5,000 (including Babe Ruth, who broke down) paid their respects to the Hall of Famer. The flags at Yankee Stadium were flown at half-mast along with the Polo Grounds, Ebbets Field, and every ballpark in the American League. In Cooperstown, the plaque bearing Gehrig's name was draped in black and stayed that way for 30 days. The funeral was the next day, and it was less than 10 minutes and featured no eulogy. Gehrig's body was cremated, and his ashes were turned over to his widow, Eleanor.

There has been some progress in the fight against ALS, but a cure has yet to be found.

Gehrig was the first famous ballplayer to be afflicted with the disease, but in 1999 former Yankee and Hall of Fame pitcher Jim "Catfish" Hunter also lost his life to Amyotrophic Lateral Sclerosis.

Mickey Mantle: Could He Have Been the Greatest?

He was born to play baseball on October 20, 1931. He was a rare combination of speed, power, and athleticism. His swing, from either side of the plate, was majestic. His trip around the bases following a home run was like royalty surveying his subjects. His fists clenched, the elbows by their sides, as he went into that famous trot that said, "Mickey Mantle just hit another home run." In the beginning he could run like the wind. He was a dual threat at the plate in that he could smack a dinger or lay a bunt down for a base hit. Just imagine yourself as a third baseman with Mantle at the plate. Do you play in to challenge the bunt? Defensively he could run down balls in the cavernous arena of Yankee Stadium (in Mantle's day, center field was 461 feet, right-center field was 407 feet, and left-center field was 457 feet) or throw a runner out with a cannon of an arm. Injuries curtailed numbers that could have been even more overwhelming, but if you can speculate and add some of the missed time, could Mantle have been the greatest to ever play the game?

Mickey Mantle burst upon the major league scene in 1951 when he made the Yankees out of spring training. Mantle was impressive in spurts, but he had trouble adjusting to major league pitching so the Yanks sent him back to their top farm team at Kansas City. Mickey responded by hitting .361 with 11 homers and 50 runs batted in during his minor league stint. The numbers belie how easy it was. It took a visit from his father, Mutt, to put Mantle back on track for what turned out to be a stellar career.

Mutt Mantle was a lead and zinc miner in Oklahoma, and he always wanted his son to be a big league ballplayer. Mickey was named after Mickey Cochrane, the Hall of Fame catcher. At age five,

Mickey Mantle, shown here in 1961, had the ability and the tools to go down as the greatest player of all time.

Mutt and Mickey's grandfather, Charles, got the young phenom started with switch-hitting. Charles would throw left-handed, and Mutt was a righty, so Mickey could practice and develop from both sides of the plate.

The young Mickey was an outstanding athlete excelling in baseball and football at Commerce High School. It was on the football field that his athletic life took a turn. He developed osteomyelitis (an inflammation of the bone marrow). His legs would never be the same, as his dysfunctional limbs would eventually curtail his baseball life.

Mantle began his career as a shortstop, but it was quickly discovered that he was not cut out for the position. Center field was not an option in 1951 as it was still Joe DiMaggio's territory, so Yankees manager Casey Stengel used Mantle in right field, where he wore No. 6.

(Cliff Mapes, a journeyman outfielder, wore No. 7 before Mantle. Mapes switched to No. 13 to allow Mantle to wear No. 7. Mapes wore No. 3 after Babe Ruth until that number was retired during the 1948 season.)

In Game 2 of the 1951 World Series against the New York Giants, Mantle tripped over an exposed drainpipe in right-center field at the stadium and tore cartilage in his knee. A day after the injury, Mickey's father, Mutt, took ill and eventually died of Hodgkin's Disease.

Playing at Yankee Stadium both helped and hurt Mantle's lifetime home-run totals, but, for the most part, he was able to conquer those long distances. In fact, Mantle hit 266 home runs at home while smacking 270 on the road.

In the mid-1950s, Mantle reached Hall of Fame status. In 1956 Mickey won baseball's Triple Crown as he batted .353, slammed 52 home runs, and drove home 130 to lead the league in all three categories. Mantle won two of his three Most Valuable Player awards in 1956 and 1957 and led the Yankees to seven pennants and five world championships during the 1950s.

Some of Mantle's blows were legendary. In April 1953 Mantle slammed what many believe to be the first ever tape-measure home run in Washington, an estimated 565-foot shot off the Senators' Chuck Stobbs. Reportedly the ball traveled 460 feet in the air before landing and going an additional 95 feet. (Later in the same game, Mantle bunted a ball that landed in front of second base, but he beat the throw for an infield single.)

On May 30, 1956, and May 22, 1963, Mantle nearly hit a ball completely out of Yankee Stadium. The first one came in the fifth inning of the opening game of a doubleheader against Washington. Mantle connected off Pedro Ramos for the prestigious blast. It was estimated that the ball struck a point 370 feet away and 117 feet off the ground. The second such shot was a walk-off home run in the bottom of the eleventh off Kansas City Athletics pitcher Bill Fischer, an eerily similar shot to the one nearly seven years prior.

Despite all his success, Mantle still had not completely won over the New York fans. Many believe it's because he replaced the legendary Joe DiMaggio, even though DiMaggio gracefully bowed out in 1951. But Joltin' Joe himself had not shown an acceptance of Mantle, and Mickey felt the brunt of that from the fans.

Things changed in 1960 when Roger Maris was acquired in a trade with Kansas City. Mantle was the established star, and Maris was the new kid on the block who had to prove himself to the local establishment. It came to a head in 1961 when Mantle and Maris were in a dramatic race for Babe Ruth's single-season home-run record of 60. Both Mickey and Roger were on pace to break the mark, and the fans began to show Mantle the support he had been lacking. Mantle got hurt in September and came up short with 54 home runs while Maris went on to break the record. Standing ovations became routine as Mantle led the Yankees to five straight pennants and two world titles as the 1960s began. But the beginning of the end of Mantle's illustrious career was evident. The injuries were starting to take their toll.

In June 1963 Mantle severely tore up his ankle trying to make a catch at Baltimore's Memorial Stadium and was out for two months. His first at-bat following that injury was a success. Mantle slammed a pinch-hit game-tying homer in the seventh.

By 1966 it was apparent that Mantle could not play the outfield anymore, so it was planned that he

TRIVIA

Who holds the Yankees record for hits in a single game with six?

Answers to the trivia questions are on pages 186–187.

TOP 10

All-Time Batting Average

1.	Babe Ruth	.349
2.	Lou Gehrig	.340
3.	Earle Combs	.325
4.	Joe DiMaggio	.325
5.	Derek Jeter	.317
6.	Wade Boggs	.313t
	Bill Dickey	.313t
8.	Bob Meusel	.311
9.	Don Mattingly	.307
10.	Ben Chapman	.305

would begin a new career as a first baseman. In those days, there was no designated hitter, so players moved to first base to prolong their careers. Mantle played two years at first and in May 1967 he hit his 500th home run off Baltimore's Stu Miller at Yankee Stadium.

Mantle announced his retirement in the spring of 1969. Eighteen big-league seasons had produced 536 career home runs, 1,509 RBIs, 2,415 hits, a countless number of memories, and, of course, a spot in the Hall of Fame.

Mickey's one regret when he retired was that his lifetime batting average had dropped under .300 to .298, but that was trivial in measuring his greatness. Mantle played in 12 World Series and still holds the record for the most World Series home runs with 18. He holds the Yankees record for most games played with 2,401, he hit .300 or better 10 times, and he was a 16-time All-Star (14 in the outfield and two times as a first baseman).

Mantle's No. 7 was retired on June 8, 1969, during Mickey Mantle Day ceremonies at Yankee Stadium. Those same fans who had hounded him early in his career stood and cheered as Mantle saluted them by riding around the stadium in an open golf cart.

Throughout his career, the injuries are as well noted as some of his longest home runs. Being afflicted with osteomyelitis was only the beginning. There was the torn knee cartilage during Game 2 of the 1951 World Series, but six years later, Mantle would suffer another injury that would impact him for the rest of his career. It was the 1957 Series against the Milwaukee Braves when Braves second baseman Red Schoendienst landed on Mantle's right shoulder causing damage that would linger for years. By the time the mid-1960s rolled around, Mantle's shoulder injury from 1957 was starting to wear him down.

The last four years (1965–1968) were the toughest. "It just seemed like maybe the taping, the gauze, and all that cut off the circulation," Mantle once said. "I got to where I couldn't score from second base and they had to put me on first base because I couldn't shag the flies anymore."

If you total 17 full seasons (we'll skip 1951 because he played only 96 games and was back in the minors), Mantle missed 377 games (an average of more than 21 per season). Multiply that total by an average of four at-bats per game and you have an additional 1,508 at-bats. If you take into account the average number of games missed by a player, you can slice the missed games per season in half (10) and multiply by four at-bats per game. If you multiply 40 by 17 seasons and subtract approximately 680 at-bats from the 1,508 total stated previous, Mantle would still have missed out on 800 at-bats. During his career, Mantle averaged one home run every 15 at-bats. If you divide those 800 at-bats by 15, Mantle would have hit only 50 to 55 more home runs.

There's no debating the fact that, without the injuries, Mantle would have produced even higher offensive numbers, but would those additional numbers have given him the label of best to ever play the game? It would make for an interesting debate.

Roger Maris: The Asterisk That Never Was

The dictionary defines *asterisk* as "a star-shaped symbol used chiefly to indicate an omission, a reference to a footnote, or an unattested word, sound, or affix." In 1961, Yankees outfielder Roger Maris became the most famous victim of this symbol when he dared to break Babe Ruth's single-season home-run record that had stood for 34 years.

What's even more astounding is that there never was an actual asterisk that appeared beside Maris's name in the record books. The baseball establishment deemed there was one problem with allowing Maris to carry the mantle of single-season home-run king. His team had played in eight more games than the Babe did—but Maris didn't create the schedule.

It was July 17, 1961, when Baseball Commissioner Ford Frick issued a ruling that any American League player (referring to Maris and Mickey Mantle) who broke Babe Ruth's single-season home-run record of 60 in 154 games would be credited with achieving the new mark. If that player passed Ruth with more than 154 games played, then there would be some distinction made in the record books.

That distinction (or asterisk) noted that Maris broke the record in a 162-game season, instead of 154 like Ruth. Frick was a ghost writer for Ruth and had some ties to the Sultan of Swat, prompting many to believe that was the reason he handed down this decision.

Maris had 35 home runs while Mantle had 32 on the day that Frick issued his ruling. In late July at Yankee Stadium, Maris blasted four home runs in a doubleheader sweep of the Chicago White Sox to reach 40 for the season. It also put the Fargo, North Dakota, native 27 games ahead of Ruth's 1927 pace.

In late August the left-hand-hitting slugger had 48 and was still 16 games ahead of the Babe, while Mantle had 45 home runs and was 14 games up.

The Yankees were in the midst of a 13-game road trip on a stopover in Los Angeles when Maris hit number 50 off Angels pitcher Ken McBride to become the first player in history to hit his 50th homer before September 1. Maris's home run came in the team's 124th game while Ruth did not hit his 50th home run until the 138th game of the 1927 season. So, according to Frick, Maris had 30 games left to break the record without any "distinctions" attached.

The season moved into September with Maris needing only nine more long balls to tie. On September 2, Maris thrilled more than 50,000 fans at the stadium with another power display as he compiled his seventh game with two home runs en route to a 7–2 win over noted Yankees killer Frank Lary and the Detroit Tigers. Maris had 20 games until the 154 game mark, needing seven more homers to tie and eight more to break the record. The countdown was on and so was the stress on Maris, who was beginning to feel the pressure of the asterisk.

Maris was already getting testy with the constant media bombardment. As the season wound down, things got worse as the left-handed slugger was reportedly losing hair due to the stress of the daily pursuit.

On September 9 the Yankees staged Whitey Ford Day and Maris made his contribution to the festivities with his 56th home run. The incumbent Most Valuable Player was six games ahead of Ruth and still had 12 to go to reach 154.

The schedule was not kind to the pursuers. Maris, Mantle, and the Yankees faced a stretch of three doubleheaders, a total of seven games in six days. It was a grueling portion of the campaign and it showed as Maris did not hit a single home run for the seven-game stretch. That left five games to go to reach 154, and Maris stood at 56. Mantle was struggling as

TRIVIA

The score of Don Larsen's perfect game in Game 5 of the 1956 Series was 2–0. Mickey Mantle drove in one run with a home run. Who drove in the other run?

Answers to the trivia questions are on pages 186–187.

TOP 10

All-Time Home Runs

1.	Babe Ruth	659
2.	Mickey Mantle	536
3.	Lou Gehrig	493
4.	Joe DiMaggio	361
5.	Yogi Berra	358
6.	Bernie Williams	287
7.	Graig Nettles	250
8.	Don Mattingly	222
9.	Dave Winfield	205
10.	Roger Maris	203

well as he was stuck on 53 and had not homered in four straight games. The Yankees were in Detroit on September 16, and Maris ended his drought with a home run off Lary, his 57th that bounded off the roof atop the upper deck in right-center field at Tiger Stadium. On the "Frick counter," Maris was down to four. Number 58 would come the next day, but Maris would go homer-less in a twin bill in Baltimore as the schedule reached 153 games played.

Mantle's attempt to break Ruth's record ended on September 20 when he entered the hospital with a debilitating virus. The former American League MVP finished the regular season with 54 dingers.

Game 154 was the coup de grâce of Maris's emotionally draining chance at Ruth's record. In the third inning, Maris hit number 59 off Orioles right-hander Milt Pappas. In the seventh he flirted with number 60 when he smacked a foul ball deep down the right-field line. In the ninth, Maris faced knuckleball pitcher Hoyt Wilhelm. Maris fouled off the first pitch and hit another drive foul down the right-field line on the second pitch. The chase ended when Maris bounced the third pitch back to Wilhelm who fielded it near the first-base bag and tagged him out.

Earlier in the year Maris had a home run in Baltimore, but the game was rained out. Even if that game had counted, that would've added another game to the schedule—so he still would not have set the mark within the Frick-imposed limit. Maris did not tie Ruth in 154 games. The only solace from the game was the fact that the Yankees clinched their second-straight and 26th American League pennant.

According to the commissioner, Maris came up short, but in reality the schedule did show eight more games to play. After going three more games without a home run, number 60 finally came. Maris connected off the Orioles' Jack Fisher in the third inning, a shot that soared into the third deck of the right-field stands,

Roger Maris watches the flight of his record-tying 60th home run on September 26, 1961, in New York.

bounced into the box seats some four rows back, and bounded back onto the field. The ball was retrieved and handed to the Yankees bench while Maris circled the bases. A surprisingly small crowd of more than 19,000 implored the slugger to take his first "curtain call." Afterward, the shy Maris would say only, "This is easily the greatest thrill of my life." Maris had two more at-bats to try to set a new mark, but he came up short.

With three games left, Maris tried to reach 61, but he went 0 for 2 with two walks against Bill Monbouquette and the Red Sox.

The next day Maris went 1 for 3 but still no home run, so it came down to the final day of the regular season. The historic home run came in the fourth inning off Red Sox right-hander Tracy Stallard on a 2–0 pitch. The memorable drive was caught in right field in section 33, box 163D, by a 19-year-old truck driver named Sal Durante. Maris left the dugout in the bottom of the fifth to meet Durante, who wanted to give the ball up for free, despite a $5,000 offer for the ball from a California restaurant owner.

The only downer of the day was that the slugger had failed to meet the Frick-imposed limit of 154 games for a new record to officially be set. So what if Maris hit his 61st home run in the Yanks' 162nd game? It became a debate that lasted for nearly 30 years.

In the clubhouse following the game, Maris put the sanction into perspective. "Naturally I'm happy that I got past that 60 during the season," Maris said. "And now that the 61st wasn't hit in 154 games, I'm happy. That's the way it was to be, and that's the way it is."

Finally, in September 1991, baseball commissioner Fay Vincent chaired a committee of statistical accuracy and declared that any notation on Maris's mark should be eliminated. Vincent's gesture may have been a tad late. According to the *Macmillan Baseball Encyclopedia,* in 1968 the special baseball records committee ruled that "for all-time single-season records, no asterisk, or official sign, shall be used to indicate the number of games scheduled."

There was 34-year gap between Ruth and Maris, but 37 more years passed until the Cardinals' Mark McGwire topped the Yankees outfielder in 1998. Consider that McGwire held the mark for only three years until Barry Bonds set a new record with 73 home runs in 2001.

The End of an Era in the Bronx

The Yankees lost the 1964 World Series in seven games to the St. Louis Cardinals, but the Yankees fans' chant, "wait till next year," meant that the fans hoped that the 1964 season was merely a bump in the road on the way to another championship. After all, the Yankees had won the American League pennant for five straight years.

But the 1965 season brought much change to the Bronx. There was a new manager in Johnny Keane, who replaced Yogi Berra. Seven months earlier, Keane had managed the Cardinals to the era-ending Series win. Legendary players like Mickey Mantle and Whitey Ford were succumbing to age and wearing down physically. Ford came off an operation to improve the blood circulation in his left arm and was 36 years old. Mantle's problematic legs were getting worse, and he began the season in left field, not center. Except for Mantle's move to left, the Opening Day lineup that took the field in Minnesota was pretty much the same one that had won the American League pennant the year before.

When the season hit the annual All-Star break in July, the Yankees were struggling at 41–46, a seventh-place standing, 14½ games behind the first-place Minnesota Twins. The five-time American League champions were in trouble—and it wasn't going to get better any time soon.

The lineup had drastically turned over in a matter of months. Familiar names like Mantle, Maris, and Kubek were replaced with other unknown monikers like Roy White, Roger Repoz, and Horace Clarke. The Yankees were all but eliminated in early September following a doubleheader loss to Baltimore at the stadium.

There was not much to gain for the former champs, but some personal milestones were set on the final weekend. Mel Stottlemyre became a 20-game winner for the first time as he beat Boston with a 6–4 complete-game victory. On the final day, Whitey Ford became the Yankees' all-time winningest pitcher when he beat the Red Sox for his 16th win of the season and the 232nd of his career, which bested Red Ruffing's total of 231.

The Yankees finished the 1965 season in sixth place with a 77–85 record, 25 games behind. Despite rumors to the contrary, Keane returned as manager to begin the 1966 season, but the Yankees had him on a short leash. It wouldn't be long before changes were again in the works. Things only got worse in 1966. The team came stumbling "out of the blocks" with a 4–16 record, and on May 7, Keane was fired as manager and replaced with general manager and former field boss Ralph Houk.

Mel Stottlemyre, a 20-game winner in 1965, was one of the few bright spots as the franchise slid into mediocrity.

IF ONLY . . . Mariano Rivera had not made that throwing error to set up Arizona's ninth-inning comeback in Game 7 of the 2001 World Series. The only way to speculate what would've happened without the error is to reconfigure the inning with the error as an out.

Instead of runners at first and second with nobody out, Arizona would have a runner at first with one man out. Assuming Rivera went on to retire Jay Bell for the second out, Tony Womack's double probably would still have tied up the game. Rivera then hit Craig Counsell with a pitch, and Luis Gonzalez might have driven home the winning run, although he would not have been batting with the infield in as he ended up doing with only one man out because of the error.

On September 18, in front of just over 12,000 fans at a dreary Yankee Stadium, the Yankees dropped into last place for the first time after a 10 inning, 5–3 loss to Minnesota. The Yankees closed out their worst home season (35–46) since they opened the stadium in 1923 as they finished in last place with a 70–89 mark. Houk continued to try and upgrade the team, but the barren farm system and a lack of quality trade material left the club to waddle through a number of non-championship seasons.

Clarke, who was the starting second baseman from 1967 to 1973, said it was tough to wear the pinstripes because there were such high standards to live up to. "This city has been spoiled," Clarke said at a recent gathering of Yankees old timers. "The winning tradition was hard to deal with."

In 1968 the Yankees finished over .500 but were 20 games out of first.

In 1969 baseball expanded the American and National Leagues into two divisions. The Bombers were 80–81, but it seemed like no one in New York knew they even existed as the crosstown rival New York Mets pulled off their "miracle" world championship run.

Nineteen seventy provided a bit of a surprise as the Yankees won 93 games but finished second, 15 back of the eventual world champion Baltimore Orioles. Nineteen seventy-one brought a fourth-place finish, but in 1972 the Yankees found themselves in a real pennant race.

On Thursday, August 10, the Yankees hosted the first-place Detroit Tigers in the finale of a four-game series. New York was in third place in the American League East, trailing Detroit by only three games. A crowd of more than 45,000 was on hand. It had been a long time since the stadium saw a turnout like that for a weeknight game. A pair of 12-game winners put on a good old-fashioned pitchers' duel as Detroit's Joe Coleman battled New York's Steve Kline. The Yanks scored a run on a Johnny Callison RBI single in the fourth, and Kline made it stand up by tossing eight scoreless innings. It was 1–0 going to the top of the ninth and the sounds of "Pomp and Circumstance" were heard on the stadium's loudspeakers. That was Sparky Lyle's entrance theme, and the crowd responded to the Yankees closer as he stepped out of the bullpen car and onto the mound. (In those days, the relievers were driven in from the bullpen in a sponsored automobile.) Lyle struck out pinch hitter Ike Brown with the bases loaded, and the Yankees had a scintillating victory.

Yankees reliever Sparky Lyle poses with his Life Saver of the Month Award in July 1973.

On September 12, the Yankees were tied with Baltimore for second, only a half game behind the first-place Red Sox. But the club proceeded to lose six of their next seven games, which left them four and a half games back with only 10 games left. The Yankees were three and a half out with five games left, but they closed a promising season on a sour note, dropping their final five games to finish in fourth place, six and a half games out of first.

Houk (aka "the Major" for his marine exploits in World War II) ran the team for one more season. His final game was also the final game played at the original Yankee Stadium. Following the season, and after a reported falling out with new owner George Steinbrenner, Houk resigned from the Yankees and took the managerial job with Detroit for the 1974 season.

The Yankees were headed to Shea Stadium for the 1974 campaign, and they were bringing along a new field boss in Bill Virdon. A second-place finish in 1974 preceded a third-place standing in 1975 (see "Chez Yankees") before Chris Chambliss finally ended the drought with his famous walk-off, pennant-winning home run (see "Pinstripe Glory") in 1976.

By the NUMBERS

22—Number of innings in the longest game in Yankees history. On June 24, 1962, the Yankees scored a 9–7 win at Detroit, thanks to a two-run home run by Jack Reed in the top of the twenty-second inning.

"Chez Yankees": Yankees Would Play at Shea in 1974 and 1975

It was Tuesday, August 8, 1972. The Yankees won a 4–2 decision from the Detroit Tigers at Yankee Stadium, but the real news was made earlier that day. The Yankees announced the signing of a 30-year agreement with New York City to play in a remodeled Yankee Stadium beginning with the 1976 season.

In the late 1960s and early 1970s, rumors began circulating about a renovation for the 49-year-old ballpark. The structure was beginning to deteriorate, the parking areas were becoming obsolete, and the Yankees were falling behind the times when it came to their home.

The team would play its final season at the ballpark in the south Bronx in 1973. It was determined (with the cooperation of the New York Mets) that the Yankees would play their home games for the 1974 and 1975 seasons at Shea Stadium in Queens, New York, while Yankee Stadium was being renovated. Thus began a two-year period that would reshape the team on and off the field for years to come.

On April 6, 1974, the Yankees played their first game at Shea as the home team defeated the Cleveland Indians 6–1 behind Mel Stottlemyre's complete-game victory before an announced crowd of 20,744. Future Hall of Famer and Indians pitcher Gaylord Perry, who was known for using the "spitter," was found to have thrown one in the sixth inning with Graig Nettles at bat. (Perry later admitted to having first used the "spitball" in a 1964 game at Shea against the Mets.) An interesting side note to the game was the fact that the starting first baseman for the Indians that day was Chris Chambliss.

Twenty days later, Chambliss would be dealt to the Yankees as part of a seven-player deal. The Indians received pitchers Fred Beene,

Tom Buskey, Steve Kline, and Fritz Peterson in exchange for Chambliss and pitchers Dick Tidrow and Cecil Upshaw. It would prove to be one of the significant trades in the history of the franchise.

On April 27, Chambliss made his Yankees debut at Shea Stadium and went 1 for 4 in a 6–1 loss to the Texas Rangers. As the season wore on, the Yankees made a surprising run for the American

Chris Chambliss was traded to the Yankees from Cleveland in 1974 and went on to hit one of the more famous home runs in Yankees history. Photo courtesy of MLB Photos via Getty Images.

League Eastern Division crown. With 18 games remaining, the Yankees had a two and a half game lead on second-place Boston and a three game lead on the third-place Orioles. The schedule brought the Yanks and Orioles together for the final time in a three-game midweek series at Shea.

A crowd of 33,784 saw the Orioles' Jim Palmer shut down the Bombers on seven hits in a complete-game (4–0) victory that moved the Birds to within a game and a half.

TRIVIA

In 1929 the Yankees became the first team to make numbers a permanent part of their uniform. In that season, what player, who would go on to become a colorful manager, wore No. 7 because he batted seventh in the lineup?

Answers to the trivia questions are on pages 186–187.

Baltimore took the second game and put the finishing touches on a sweep as lefty Dave McNally tossed a three hitter in the Orioles' 7–0 rout. With the three-game wipeout, the Birds took a half game lead over the Bombers in the AL East. The Yanks had 12 games left to make up the deficit.

A three-game sweep of Cleveland allowed the Bombers to stay alive and trail Baltimore by a half game with just two to play. The scheduling for the final series saw the Yankees in Milwaukee against the Brewers while the Orioles finished the regular season in Detroit. Baltimore won their opener against the Tigers to push the Yankees' deficit to a full game.

The division race, however, would not come down to the final day. The Orioles beat Detroit 7–6 on Andy Etchebarren's pinch-hit, RBI double, while the Yankees would lose in Milwaukee 3–2 on George Scott's walk-off, game-winning, RBI single. Bill Virdon's Yankees finished in second place with an 89–73 mark.

In their first year at Shea Stadium, the Yankees would come closer to a postseason berth than they did in their final 10 years at the pre-1976 Yankee Stadium.

In late 1974 the Yankees added two significant chips to enhance their chances of winning in 1975. First, on October 22 the Yankees traded center fielder Bobby Murcer to the San Francisco Giants for outfielder Bobby Bonds. Then on New Year's Eve, the Yankees announced the signing of free-agent pitcher Catfish

Hunter. The Yankees were optimistic heading into the 1975 season, their second and final one at Shea. With Bonds and Hunter on board, and the team coming up just short in 1974, the Yankees felt 1975 would be their year to return to the top. Things didn't start too well, however.

The Yankees lost their first three games, including Hunter's debut in Game 2 where he went the distance but came up on the short end of a 5–3 game against the Detroit Tigers at Shea. Tigers first baseman Nate Colbert's three-run homer was the deciding blow. Yankees right-hander Doc Medich tossed a two-hit shutout against Detroit for the Yanks' first win, but they went on to lose the next three to start the season at 1–6.

Hunter won his first game in a Yankees uniform on April 27 at Shea as he three-hit the Milwaukee Brewers.

A six-game losing streak left the Bombers in last place at 10–16, six games back of the front-running Milwaukee Brewers in the American League East.

On May 30 the Bombers were 20–24, four games back from first-place Boston, when they went on an eight-game winning streak. On the final day before the break, the Yankees played a wild game against Minnesota at Shea that didn't end, but instead was suspended. (See the "Top Ten Strangest Regular Season Games" list.) The game was later completed in Minnesota.

The Yankees entered the All-Star break trailing Boston by four games. The second half of the season didn't start too well as the club lost two in a row out of the gate, including a tough 1–0 loss to Gaylord Perry and the Texas Rangers that left the Yanks six games behind Boston.

Entering play on July 24 the Yankees faced a killer, four-day stretch of games beginning with a doubleheader at Chicago against the White Sox. The Bombers got swept in the twin bill at Comiskey Park.

Next up, a crucial four-game series with Boston at Shea that ended with a doubleheader. The Yankees needed to get at least three out of four because they trailed the Red Sox by eight games. After winning the opener of the series 8–6, the rivals were tied at one heading into the ninth of the second game, but Boston broke the deadlock with three runs and held on for a huge 4–2 victory.

TOP 10

All-Time Earned-Run Average

1.	Russ Ford	2.54
2.	Jack Chesbro	2.58
3.	Al Orth	2.72
4.	Ernie Bonham	2.73
5.	Whitey Ford	2.75
6.	Spud Chandler	2.84
7.	Ray Fisher	2.91
8.	Mel Stottlemyre	2.97
9.	Ray Caldwell	3.00
10.	Bob Shawkey	3.10†
	Fritz Peterson	3.10†
	Stan Bahnsen	3.10†

On Sunday, the Sox swept the twin bill from the Yankees that just about ended their chances for winning the East as they fell 10 games back.

The opener was an emotional 1–0 defeat, keyed by a spectacular defensive play from Bosox center fielder Fred Lynn. The Yankees had their chances against ol' friend Bill Lee, including a bases-loaded, no-out situation in the fifth where they failed to score.

After Boston scored an unearned run in the top of the ninth, Lynn robbed Graig Nettles of a sure double and maybe a triple with a diving catch in left-center field. That play drained the Yankees' emotions, and it showed in the nightcap as they were shut out on six hits by Boston's Rogelio Moret.

The Yanks would never recover, and changes were in the works. Rumors of a managerial shake-up were already being tossed around. Anonymous quotes about the way Bill Virdon was running the club began to surface. Billy Martin was available, and Yankees owner George Steinbrenner had always been fond of the enigmatic skipper. After a stirring 5–4 win over Cleveland on Friday night, August 1, Virdon was dismissed and replaced with Martin. The Yanks were 53–51, still 10 games back. They were hoping that Billy the Kid would provide a late-season spark. It wasn't to be. Problems mounted,

TRIVIA

In the infamous pine tar game against Kansas City in 1983, Goose Gossage gave up George Brett's home run, but when the game resumed in August, who was the Yankees pitcher who got the final out in the top of the ninth?

Answers to the trivia questions are on pages 186–187.

which destroyed any hope of pulling out the division title.

Left fielder Lou Piniella was dealing with an inner-ear infection that ruined his season and actually prevented the Yankees from dealing him to the Angels in a trade for second baseman Denny Doyle. Reliever Sparky Lyle and pitcher Doc Medich were both having down years while Catfish Hunter was finding it too difficult to carry the load for the staff.

The Yankees' final day at Shea featured a doubleheader against the Orioles. In the opener, Hall of Famer Jim Palmer shut out the Yanks on eight hits, but the nightcap ended on a positive note as the club rallied for three runs in the bottom of the ninth to score a 3–2 victory before more than 20,000 die-hard fans.

Southpaw Larry Gura went the distance to become the Yanks' final winning pitcher at Shea. Rich Coggins was the final Yankees batter, but he never got an at-bat because an error by Orioles pitcher Dyar Miller on a pickoff attempt of Rick Dempsey at third allowed the winning run to score.

The Yankees finished the 1975 season in third place with an 83–77 record, 12 games behind the first-place Red Sox. The Yankees would play one more time at Shea as a home team during the 1998 season. Because of a structural problem at the stadium, the Yankees were allowed to move a scheduled game against the Anaheim Angels to Shea Stadium. On the afternoon of April 15, 1998, the Yankees beat the Angels 6–3. That night, the Mets hosted the Chicago Cubs in a real nightcap.

Reggie's Three-Home-Run Night: Vindication

The euphoria from Chris Chambliss's pennant-winning home run to beat Kansas City in the 1976 American League championship had barely begun to wear off when the Yankees found themselves in Cincinnati for game one of the Series.

When it was over you thought to yourself, *Whoa, what just happened? Were they really in a World Series?* It was like a punch to the stomach. Despite ending a 12-year stretch without postseason play, as a Yankees fan, you still had a feeling of incompleteness. It didn't totally ruin the season, but it jolted you into realizing that the Yankees were still one piece short. That missing piece came wrapped up in a free-agent package named Reggie Jackson. Here was the player that the Yanks needed—a left-handed power threat who was already a member of three world championship teams. I (the author) was already a huge Reggie fan. I had followed his accomplishments with the Oakland A's and was hoping he would be traded to the Yankees in 1976. A's owner Charles O. Finley put Jackson on the trade block, but instead of sending him to New York he dealt the slugger to Baltimore as part of a six-player deal. Once the season ended, Jackson filed for free agency, and in November 1976 the Yankees signed Jackson to a five-year contract. Of course, I was ecstatic.

The problem was that in my Bronx neighborhood not everybody was a Reggie Jackson fan. I spent the entire 1977 baseball season defending a man whom I had never met, never had any contact with on a personal level, and I tried to convince a bunch of skeptics that this was the person who would help the Yankees get back to the promised land.

TOP 10

World Series Pitching Performances by a Yankee

1. **October 8, 1956:** Larsen's perfect game
2. **October 1961–October 1962:** Whitey Ford's Series-record 33⅔ innings scoreless streak
3. **October 16, 1962:** Ralph Terry goes the distance on a four hitter to capture a 1–0 victory in the seventh game in San Francisco
4. **October 8, 1964:** Rookie pitcher Mel Stottlemyre goes the distance in Game 2 win over Cards
5. **October 9, 1958:** Bob Turley tosses six-plus innings of one-run relief in Game 7 versus Milwaukee to nail down the Series and Most Valuable Player award
6. **October 13, 1978:** Ron Guidry goes the distance in key Game 3 win over the Dodgers
7. **October 24, 1996:** Andy Pettitte pitches into the ninth in 1–0, Game 5 win in final tilt at Atlanta's Fulton County Stadium
8. **October 23, 1999:** Orlando "El Duque" Hernandez goes seven for Game 1 win, strikes out 10
9. **October 15, 1978:** A much-maligned Jim Beattie goes all the way to win key Game 5 for Yanks
10. **October 1952:** Allie Reynolds, starter and reliever, earns two wins and a save and tosses more than 20 innings in victory over Brooklyn

Ah! It was time for spring training and I, for one, could not wait. I was anxious to see Jackson put on the pinstripes. Did he hit any home runs in his first batting practice? How were the swings? These questions would be put to the newest Yankee at their Fort Lauderdale complex, but they would not compare to the questions he and I would have to answer for the infamous article that appeared in *Sport Magazine*.

People already knew about the comments he made in reference to Thurman Munson. The famous quote was "I'm the straw that stirs the drink." There it was, in black and white, for all to see, including Munson and the rest of his teammates who felt Jackson was wrong to imply that he would step right in and lead the team. It set an odious tone at the beginning of the season in which all parties got off on the wrong foot.

Game 2 brought the first crisis as Jackson's failure to catch a fly ball led to three unearned runs and a 3–2 loss to Milwaukee at the stadium.

"Did you see what the millionaire did? Can't even catch a cold," was the mantra offered by the neighborhood crowd. Eating crow became a steady habit early in the year, and I was feeling the pain.

Jackson hit his first Yankees home run in the fourth game off of Kansas City southpaw Paul Splittorff, but the Bombers lost to the Royals. Since it was his first year in pinstripes, Jackson was trying hard to impress, but his numbers were way down. After one month, Jackson only had three home runs and 11 runs batted in.

I could hear it. A beautiful sunny morning in May was going to be ruined by those doomsday prophets saying that Jackson was overrated.

At the All-Star break, Reggie had 16 home runs and 50 runs batted in. Not bad, but certainly not superstar statistics, so Jackson was, according to many "experts," underachieving.

The Yankees were in third place, three games behind Boston and a game and a half behind Baltimore, and Jackson had not even gotten hot yet. Or at least, I hoped he hadn't.

The second verse was the same as the first as Jackson struggled to get going. My struggles were just beginning as I began to take abuse (good-natured, but nonetheless unnerving) for backing this supposed star. One thing that I wasn't getting through all of this was why Yankees manager Billy Martin insisted on keeping Jackson out of the fourth spot in the batting order. It made perfect sense. Jackson could hit cleanup behind a terrific number-three hitter in Munson. Martin claimed that Jackson struck out too much so he didn't want him hitting fourth. But on August 10, the Hall of Fame outfielder went into the four hole—and the Yankees never looked back. Thirteen home runs and 49 RBIs in the final 51 games catapulted the Yankees to their second-straight Eastern Division crown.

TOP 10

World Series Hitting Performances by a Yankee

1. **October 16, 1977:** Reggie Jackson slams three home runs in Game 6 as Yanks clinch 21st World Series by beating the Dodgers
2. **October 10, 1964:** Mickey Mantle's walk-off home run to beat Barney Schultz and the Cardinals in Game 3
3. **October 1976:** Thurman Munson hits .529 (highest by a Yankee in a single Series) in four-game sweep by Reds
4. **October 1, 1932:** Babe Ruth's "called shot" against the Cubs in Game 3
5. **October 1960:** Bobby Richardson drives in 12 runs in a losing cause, still wins MVP
6. **October 2000:** Derek Jeter becomes 18th Yankee to win Series MVP while slamming a momentum-shifting home run to lead off Game 4
7. **October 1953:** Billy Martin bats .500 (12 for 24, two home runs, eight RBIs in six games) to win the Series Most Valuable Player award
8. **October 1951:** Phil Rizzuto wins Series MVP (8 for 25 in six games, one home run, three RBIs)
9. **October 6, 1926:** Babe Ruth hits three home runs, scores four, and drives in four in Game 4
10. **October 14, 1923:** Joe Dugan goes 4 for 5 with a home run and three RBIs in Game 5

On October 1 the Yankees clinched their second straight division title, and it was on to the American League championship series.

"So what, they were there last year," said my neighborhood buddies.

"With Reggie, they're better than last year," I retorted.

It took a very short time for that feeling to disappear. The teams split the first two at Yankee Stadium with Games 3, 4, and 5 set for Kansas City. The Royals grabbed Game 3, putting all the pressure on the Yankees who needed to win two straight on the road or the season would be wasted. It didn't help that Jackson was having a lousy series. Reggie was 1 for 14 in the first four games, and on the afternoon of Game 5, I was simply hoping that Jackson was due. As I awaited the start of the game, I was stunned to hear that Jackson had been benched by Billy Martin against the Royals' tough left-hander Splittorff.

What the...Jackson benched? What is Martin thinking? I thought to myself. *You bring the guy here to get you back to the World Series, and you're benching him in the biggest game of the season!*

Martin was taking an enormous gamble that looked even worse when Kansas City took a 3–1 lead after three innings. The score stood up until the eighth when Jackson made his presence felt. With runners at first and third, the future Hall of Famer pinch hit for Cliff Johnson and stroked a run-scoring single to center to cut the deficit to 3–2. That hit set the stage for the ninth-inning comeback as the Yankees scored three times and held off the Royals 5–3 to earn a trip back to the World Series.

Jackson was partially vindicated. He had come through in a big spot when the Yanks really needed it. At least, that's how I put it the next morning against the neighborhood debating team. Next up, the World Series.

The first three games were just like the season. A 2-for-9 showing with no homers and one RBI. I heard the cynics, full blast. "Told you so. The guy's not clutch," they said. "Oh yeah?" I answered back, "What about with Oakland?" Luckily the Yanks led the Series 2–1 and from then on it was smooth sailing.

Jackson came alive going 2 for 4 in Game 4 with his first home run followed by another 2 for 4 and a second home run. The Yanks lost Game 5 but returned to New York with a 3–2 lead and a chance to wrap it up at home.

Jackson was hot, I thought. *Maybe he'll do something tonight.* I couldn't wait for it to start. I even took the chance of inviting the doubters over to my place to watch the game.

First at-bat, a walk on four pitches, and he scored on Chris Chambliss's two-run homer. Two to zip, Yanks, and we were on our way.

Reggie Jackson connects for his third home run during Game 6 of the 1977 World Series against the Dodgers at Yankee Stadium.

In the fourth, Jackson hit a two-run homer, and I hit the roof. They brought Reggie in to help win the World Series and by golly, the guy was getting it done.

Next at-bat, another two-run homer. Reggie hit two, and the silence coming from my viewing partners was deafening. Was it too much to ask for three?

Jackson led off the eighth, and the crowd was already standing and roaring, not only for the two home runs he'd already put in the bank, but they were also hoping for another encore.

Knuckleballer Charlie Hough delivered his flutter, and Jackson entered an exclusive club of Yankees greats as he deposited the knuckler in "the black" of the unoccupied center-field bleachers. My time had come. All those support sessions, all the aggravation of defending the man, all the anxious moments. It was all worth it. The Yankees had another championship. I turned to my friends with a look of total satisfaction.

The Comeback

As they entered the 1978 campaign with hopes of repeating as World Series champions, the Yankees never imagined the kind of season that was about to unfold. It was a roller-coaster ride of great proportions that led to the greatest comeback in team history.

Changes were made after Reggie Jackson slammed three home runs to cap off the 1977 World Series.

Despite the fact that closer Sparky Lyle became the first American League reliever to win the coveted Cy Young Award in 1977, flame-throwing right-hander Goose Gossage was signed as a free agent. This created a little friction among the members of the club who showed their loyalty to the colorful left-hander, and it showed as the team got off to a slow start. By mid-May, injuries had plagued the roster, and the Yankees were not able to play up to their potential.

While injury problems and just bad play continued to haunt the Yankees, the Boston Red Sox were surging. Boston got off to a very fast start as they won their 50th game on June 25. At the break, the Yankees were a respectable 46–38, but they were in third place, 11½ games behind the front-running Red Sox who were a phenomenal 57–26 at the halfway point.

The Yankees stumbled out of the break losing four of five, but they rallied to go on a five-game winning streak capped off by a 3–1 win in Chicago.

That was the final game for Billy Martin as the Yankees manager. There had been growing sentiment among the Yankees brass that Martin was losing the team's respect. The Yankees were trailing the

GOOD THING . . . Lou Piniella was able to overcome a blinding Boston sun to snag Jerry Remy's single and keep Rick Burleson from going to third in the ninth inning of the 1978 playoff game. The Yankees would've lost one of the most important games in their entire history if Piniella hadn't made the catch. Piniella's play became even more important when the next hitter, Jim Rice, flied out deep to right. Burleson could only take third and Goose Gossage got Carl Yastrzemski to foul out to third.

Red Sox by double digits and things did not seem to be improving. Not only that, but Martin's authority was being challenged by one of his star players.

On July 17, in a game against Kansas City, Jackson was given a bunt sign by Martin on the first pitch of a key at-bat. Martin took the bunt off, but Jackson bunted anyway. The Yankees backed Martin on a count of insubordination, and they suspended Jackson for five games. The beleaguered slugger returned to the team, but Martin took it upon himself to utter the infamous quote referring to Jackson and owner George Steinbrenner that ultimately led to his dismissal. "The two of them deserve each other," said Martin. "One's a born liar; the other's convicted."

On July 24, on the balcony of the Crown Central Hotel in Kansas City, Martin announced his tearful resignation.

Former Yankees pitching coach Bob Lemon was named to replace Martin and got his first win as Yankees manager when Ron Guidry tossed a six-hit shutout to post his 15th victory against only one defeat.

Lemon and Martin were strikingly different personalities. Martin was the fiery type, always looking for an edge. He was a brilliant strategist, but sometimes he was overly emotional. Lemon was just the opposite. He was laid-back, a real player's manager, and it seemed to provide the tonic that the Yankees needed. But the two did have something in common. A left-hander who was putting together the greatest single season by a Yankees pitcher in franchise history.

Ron Guidry was single-handedly keeping the Yankees in the race. The team had some kind of good karma going each time Louisiana

Lightning took the mound. There was pressure because the Yankees had to make up a lot of ground on Boston and could not afford many more losses the rest of the year.

"I knew what was being called upon me," Guidry said. "I didn't give up very many runs that season." The team appeared to be coming together as they approached a short two-game series with Boston in early August, trailing the Sox by six and a half games.

In the opener, the Yankees built a 5–0 lead after three, but the Red Sox battled back to make it a 5–4 game in the sixth. After a 35-minute rain delay in the top of the eighth, Boston tied the game off Gossage on a sacrifice fly by Carl Yastrzemski. Goose tossed seven innings in the game, but it remained tied in the bottom of the fourteenth, when Reggie Jackson's strikeout ended the inning at 1:16 AM Eastern Time. The American League curfew went into effect and the game was resumed the next day, before the regularly scheduled game, beginning with the top of the fifteenth.

The game stayed tied until the seventeenth inning when Red Sox shortstop Rick Burleson and left fielder Jim Rice stroked run-scoring singles to give Boston a 7–5 lead. The Yankees went quietly against Bob Stanley, and the Bombers had a deflating loss that left them seven and a half games back. Despite the emotional defeat, the team still had to play the regularly scheduled contest.

Weather problems played a role as the Red Sox scored a rain-shortened, seven-inning, 8–1 victory behind former Yankee Mike Torrez, who allowed an unearned run in six innings of work. The Yankees were crushed. Eight and a half back, 9 in the loss column with 55 games left. Things looked bleak.

The emotional hangover carried over to the next game as Guidry lost for only the second time all year, a 2–1 loss to Baltimore at Yankee Stadium. After that setback things began to turn around.

The Bombers went on a six-game winning streak and took 10 of their next 12 to pull into second place, seven and a half games back.

A minor slip-up occurred as the club dropped two of three to the Mariners in Seattle, but they closed the month of August on a tear, winning eight of their last nine to stand six and a half back of Boston, six in the loss column, as the teams entered the September stretch.

All-Time Team

Yankees Free-Agent Signing Team

Position	Name	Signing Date
C	John Flaherty	December 2003

Flaherty provided a strong back-up presence for Jorge Posada.

1B	Jason Giambi	December 2001

Despite some issues in his Yankees career, he did hit 40+ home runs in his first two seasons in pinstripes. He hit two big home runs off Pedro Martinez in Game 7 of the 2003 ALCS versus Boston.

2B	Mariano Duncan	December 1995

Duncan made a major contribution to the 1996 World Series.

SS	Tony Fernandez	December 1994

Fernandez became the first Yankees shortstop to hit for the cycle in 1995.

3B	Wade Boggs	December 1992

Boggs was a two-time, Gold Glove–winning third baseman for the Yanks. He drew a key walk in Game 4 of the 1996 Series and rode a horse for a victory lap at Yankee Stadium following the Game 6 win.

LF	Dave Winfield	December 1980

The Hall of Famer signed a deal that was the most lucrative ever at the time ($23 million over 10 years).

CF	Hideki Matsui	December 2002

One of the shrewdest signings ever made by the Yankees. Matsui has developed a reputation for being a terrific clutch hitter.

RF	Reggie Jackson	November 1976

Jackson helped lead the Yanks to two World Series titles; he hit three home runs in the Game 6 clincher of the 1977 Series; he is a Hall of Famer; his number (No. 44) was retired in Monument Park.

DH   Chili Davis   December 1997

Like Matsui, Davis was an underrated sign. Davis provided a switch-hitting power threat at DH and leadership in the clubhouse.

RHS   Catfish Hunter   December 1974

The very first free agent signed by the Yankees, the Hall of Famer helped the Yanks to two World Series championships.

LHS   David Wells   December 1996

Wells tossed the second perfect game in Yankees history and was the ace of the staff on the 1998 record-setting championship team.

RHR   Goose Gossage   November 1977

Goose was an intimidator coming out of the pen. His best Yankees moment was getting Hall of Famer Carl Yastrzemski for the final out of the classic one-game playoff win over Boston in 1978.

LHR   Mike Stanton   November 1996

This free-agent left hander was very reliable coming out of the pen during the Yankees three-peat from 1998 to 2000.

Does not include players who re-signed as free agents.

The Yankees knew they had an "ace in the hole" as the schedule showed seven more games to play with the Red Sox. Four in Boston to start, with three more scheduled for New York. Before the first of those seven games with the Bosox, the Yankees played a key seven-game home stand against Seattle and Detroit.

After dropping the opener to the Mariners, the Yankees rallied to grab the next two, including the finale, which provided an extra dose of dramatics and turned into one of the pivotal wins of the great comeback. The Bombers led Seattle 4–2 going to the ninth, but Sparky Lyle gave up a run-scoring double to Bill Stein, and the Mariners had runners at second and third with nobody out when Goose Gossage was called upon to wiggle out of the jam. Gossage proceeded to strike out the next three hitters including the very tough Julio Cruz to end it, and the Yankees had an enormous one-run win.

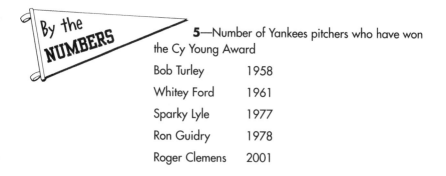

5—Number of Yankees pitchers who have won the Cy Young Award

Bob Turley	1958
Whitey Ford	1961
Sparky Lyle	1977
Ron Guidry	1978
Roger Clemens	2001

The deficit was five and a half games. The Yanks took three of the next four against Detroit to set up the showdown at Fenway. After being behind 14 games in late July, the standings read: AL East, Boston 86–52, New York 82–56.

The Yankees had made up 10 games in the standings in seven weeks and were smelling blood. The Red Sox were feeling the heat, and the Yankees were feeling like a supremely confident club heading into Game 1.

In the opener, Willie Randolph drove in five runs and the Yankees took a 12–0 lead after four en route to a 15–3 rout.

Game 2 the next night was not much different. The Yankees led 8–0 after two and the Red Sox were terrible, committing seven errors in a 13–2 disaster.

In both games, the Yankees had a starting player go three for three before the Sox went once through their lineup. A combined 28–5 score stared Boston in the face as they prepared to go against a 20–2 Guidry. Gator proceeded to throw his seventh complete game shutout of the season, a nifty two hitter as the Yanks won 7–0 to move within one game of first place. The "massacre" was completed in Game 4 as the Yankees drubbed the Red Sox 7–4 to move into a flat-footed tie for first with 20 games left. Boston retook the top spot the next day as they beat the Orioles 5–4 while the Yankees were idle.

The Yankees climbed back into first place on September 13 and would lead Boston by a game and a half as the teams prepared for a three-game showdown in New York.

For the second straight start, Guidry tossed a two-hit shutout against the Red Sox as the Yanks won 4–0 to go up two and a half games. A walk-off sacrifice fly by Thurman Munson in the bottom of the ninth of Game 2 gave the Yanks a 3–2 win, but Boston rebounded to win the series finale to get back to two and a half games out with two weeks left.

What followed was an incredible stretch by two great teams that refused to be denied.

Heading into the final eight games of the season, the Red Sox trailed the Yankees by only two games, but they would not let up one iota as they went on a tear, winning seven in a row heading into the final day of the season. Meanwhile, the Yankees continued to play well but they just couldn't keep up with the torrid pace the Bosox were setting.

The Yankees won six straight and led the Sox by one game going into the final Sunday, October 1, but the Cleveland Indians played a huge role in scripting the drama that was to occur between the two hated rivals. The Red Sox needed to win and have the Indians beat the Yankees to force a one-game playoff at Fenway Park on Monday. (A coin flip won by Boston determined the site of the game.)

Cleveland was living up to their end of the bargain as they took a 6–2 lead in New York after two innings. They had Yankees killer Rick Waits on the mound. The Sox had to use their best pitcher, Luis Tiant, to get the win in the season finale, and the colorful Cuban star did not disappoint as he tossed a two-hit shutout against the Toronto Blue Jays at Fenway.

The Sox were still playing when Yankees left fielder Roy White flied out to Cleveland's Dan Briggs in right field for the final out in New York. The score went up on the board at Fenway to a rousing standing ovation.

Left-hander Rick Waits and the Cleveland Indians had beaten the Yankees and Catfish Hunter, 9–2. Ten minutes after the Yankees final went up, Tiant got Blue Jays' third baseman Roy Howell to foul out to Boston third baseman Jack Brohamer, and a one-game playoff to determine the winner of the American League East was all set for the next afternoon.

The Yankees had set their rotation in the event of such a show-down, so 24-game-winner Ron Guidry would get the ball against Boston's Mike Torrez.

The Bombers thought they got a break because Tiant had to pitch the regular season finale. A year earlier, Torrez was the winner in Game 6 as the Yankees won their first World Series in 15 years. This time he was standing in the way of a third-straight division title.

Guidry was a cool, calm customer who did not wilt under the pressure and brought an air of confidence to his Yankees teammates when he took the mound. "Guys would start teasing me, but I was amazed how much they relied on a 150-pound guy," said Guidry.

The rest was history.

Guidry was not at his best that day, but he was good enough as he kept the Yanks in it, limiting Boston to two runs. The Yanks batted in the seventh and trailed 2–0 with two out and two on when Bucky Dent hit his famous three-run homer to turn the game around. The Yanks held a slim 5–4 lead in the bottom of the ninth. With two out

Bucky Dent hits his historic home run off Red Sox ace Mike Torrez during the 1978 playoff game between the Yankees and Boston to decide the AL Eastern Division.

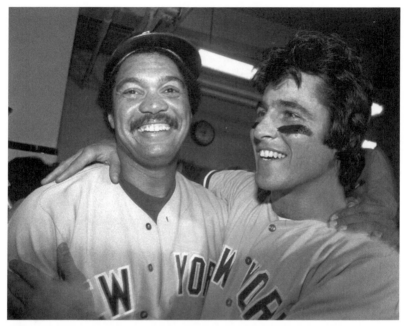

Reggie Jackson (left) and Bucky Dent celebrate New York's 5–4 win over the Red Sox on October 2, 1978, capping one of the most dramatic late-season comebacks in major league history.

and two on, Goose Gossage got Boston's Carl Yastrzemski to foul out to Graig Nettles at third. The Yankees came all the way back to win the division. They went on to beat Kansas City for the pennant and the Dodgers once again in the Series for their second consecutive world championship and 22nd championship overall.

The Day the Captain Died

The date was Thursday, August 2, 1979, a day that will live in Yankees franchise infamy. It was an off day for the Yankees but not from the reality of life. The news came in around 4:00 PM Eastern Time that afternoon. A Cessna Citation 501, registration number N15NY, crashed at 3:02 PM at the Canton-Akron airport. There were two survivors and one fatality, Thurman Munson.

The darkest day in franchise history was only the start of the most emotional five-day stretch a baseball team could ever experience. Yankees owner George Steinbrenner was the first team official to get the news. Steinbrenner received a call from Neal Callahan of the Chicago District Office of the Federal Aviation Administration, who broke the bad news. By early evening the word had spread and reactions were pouring in from all over.

Former pitcher and Yankees broadcaster Jim Kaat was a member of that 1979 Yankees team. He was living in the city at the time and learned of Munson's death on a TV news program. "You're numb for about a week," said Kaat.

The world of baseball mourned one of its own and the Yankees would grieve for the remainder of that year, as they would have to complete the 1979 season without their captain and their leader. With 56 games left to play, the Yankees were in fourth place, trailing the first-place Baltimore Orioles by 14 games. The numbers became meaningless for a ship that was rudderless.

At the time of his death, Munson was rumored to have been contemplating retirement. Eleven years of getting beat up behind the plate was taking its toll on the former Rookie of the Year. The Yankees were using Munson at different positions during the season, including first base and DH. Munson's final game as a Yankees catcher came in Milwaukee's County Stadium on July 27, less than a week before his death. The 1976 American League's Most Valuable Player played the final game of his life on August 1 at Comiskey Park against the Chicago White Sox. Munson started at first base and was 0 for 1 with a walk and a run scored. After White Sox starter Ken Kravec struck him out in the top of the third, Munson was replaced by Jim Spencer at first. Who could have imagined that it would be the last time Munson would ever be in a Yankees uniform?

"That was kinda the end of the season," Kaat said.

Yankees manager Billy Martin was crushed. "I started crying as soon as I heard," said Martin, "and I cried for hours."

Nineteen seventy-nine was already a tough year for the Bombers, but this tragedy just made every other problem seem trivial at best. "You always want to think positive," said Goose Gossage. "But it seems like not only me but everybody had that kind of year when nothing goes right." (Gossage was injured early in the season during a shower fight with catcher Cliff Johnson.) The flame-throwing right-hander put the tragedy in its proper perspective. "It's not quite like

Yankees catcher Thurman Munson is shown in 1978. Munson was killed in a plane crash on August 2, 1979.

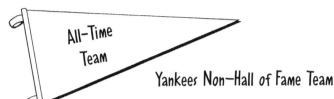

All-Time
Team

Yankees Non–Hall of Fame Team

Position   **Name**

C   Thurman Munson
Leadership, grit, and an ability to come through in the clutch personified the Yankees captain who perished in a plane crash on August 2, 1979. He was the AL Most Valuable Player in 1976. He hit .529 in the 1976 Series.

1B   Don Mattingly
Mattingly was one of the most popular Yankees of all time. For a period in the 1980s, he was considered one of the best players in baseball. He won the 1985 AL MVP award.

2B   Bobby Richardson/Willie Randolph
It's a flat-footed tie between these two Yankees greats. Both were integral parts of World Series teams and both brought intangibles that made them special Yankees players.

SS   Tony Kubek
Kubek's career was cut short by a neck injury. He won the 1957 American League Rookie of the Year award. He was involved in a famous play in the 1960 Series where a potential double-play ball hit him in the throat, leading to a five-run rally by the Pirates.

3B   Clete Boyer/Graig Nettles
Like their second-base brethren, both played on championship clubs. Nettles was the superior power hitter, but Boyer also got some big hits. Both won Gold Gloves.

LF   Roy White
One of the most underrated Yankees, White toiled through some tough times in the 1960s but tasted a championship in the late 1970s.

CF   Mickey Rivers
Rivers provided the spark for the 1976–1978 American League champions. Mick the Quick was a superior leadoff man and team catalyst. He was a quality hitter at big moments.

RF   Paul O'Neill

O'Neill was another spark plug who provided a much-needed jolt of energy to a lackluster bunch in the early 1990s. He played in four Yankees no-hitters, including two perfect games (three, if you include Tom Browning's perfecto in Cincinnati).

DH   Bobby Murcer

On June 24, 1970, Murcer homered in four consecutive at-bats that spanned the first and second games of a doubleheader.

RHS   Mel Stottlemyre

Stottlemyre was one of the all-time Yankees greats. Stottlemyre came up in 1964 and thrived in the spotlight of the postseason. He was a three-time 20-game winner and five-time All-Star.

LHS   Ron Guidry

Guidry compiled the greatest single season by any pitcher in Yankees history when he went 25–3 with a 1.78 ERA during his Cy Young Award–winning season of 1978. He was the winning pitcher in the one-game playoff against Boston.

RHR   Johnny Murphy

Murphy played in six World Series during his 12-year career. He saved 104 games for the Yankees.

MGR   Billy Martin

Martin could've been a Hall of Fame manager, but personal issues always got in the way of his success. He was a championship-winning skipper in 1977.

Current Yankees do not qualify.

losing anybody in your family," he said, "but it's the next closest thing. You live with these guys, you travel with these guys. It's almost like a family, and Thurman was like a brother to us all."

Outside the sports world, the tributes began pouring in. New York City mayor Ed Koch called Munson "the cornerstone of the Yankees." Governor Hugh Carey compared Munson to Lou Gehrig. Interestingly, Gehrig was a previous Yankees captain who also died at a very young age.

Thurman Munson is shown blocking the plate to tag out Kansas City's Fran Healy during a game in 1976.

The Yankees already knew what they were going to do. Munson's No. 15 would be retired to sit alongside the other Yankees greats. In addition, a plaque with his name would be placed on the center-field wall, and his locker would remain empty from then on.

The first game after the tragedy was Friday, August 3, at Yankee Stadium against Baltimore. "It was probably the best thing to play," said Kaat, "but nobody felt like playing."

It also marked the beginning of a four-day odyssey, unlike any other in Yankees history. The stadium was surreal that night. Munson's locker was emptied before anyone arrived that Friday night. "Big Pete [longtime club-house manager Pete Sheehy] had cleaned it out," Kaat said.

A crowd of more than 51,000 fans was on hand, not only to mourn the death of the Yankees captain, but to salute him as well. Kaat said, "It was an eerie feeling, pretty silent in the clubhouse."

The pregame ceremonies featured a prayer reading by Cardinal Terence Cooke and a stirring rendition of "America the Beautiful" by Metropolitan Opera star Robert Merrill. The Yankees were already on the field when Merrill sang, all except the catcher's box that was symbolically left empty to honor their fallen teammate. The remainder of the Yankees team and the entire Orioles squad were all on the top steps of their respective dugouts. After Merrill was finished, some of the players stood with their caps over their hearts and their heads bowed. Some shed tears, while others just stood around in disbelief.

The fans began to applaud. Stadium announcer Bob Sheppard tried to settle the moment by announcing, "And now it's time to play ball. Ladies and gentlemen, thank you for your cooperation." But the fans continued to applaud, and applaud, and applaud, and applaud. This went on for nearly 10 minutes. Munson's picture, which was on the center-field scoreboard, went off but then returned as the macabre applause continued.

Sheppard broke in again. "Thank you ladies and gentlemen. Thank you for your wonderful response." The applause lasted about another minute or so and then Yankees catcher Jerry Narron took his spot on the field and immediately became the answer to a trivia question.

"You felt for Bobby Murcer and Lou Piniella," said Kaat. "I wasn't on the team that long, but they were close to Thurman. There weren't many dry eyes that night on either side." Naturally the Yankees played the game in a daze as they dropped a 1–0 decision to Scott McGregor and the Orioles.

The Yankees moved through the weekend in a malaise. The funeral was set for Monday, August 6, in Canton, Ohio. The entire team and numerous dignitaries attended the funeral that Monday morning in Canton. Murcer and Piniella delivered moving eulogies to their departed friend. Following the burial, the team returned home to play the Orioles that night at the stadium in the finale of a four-game series.

TRIVIA

What was Don Mattingly's number when he made his major league debut in 1982?

Answers to the trivia questions are on pages 186–187.

Ron Guidry got the start, the first time he pitched after the tragedy. "The first time that I got to the mound and I looked around, there was something missing," said Guidry of his former battery mate. The Yankees left-hander went the distance in the game, but the night belonged to Munson's good friend Bobby Murcer. Murcer experienced a renaissance in his return to the club in late June.

The Yankees dug themselves a 4–0 hole, but just as if the Captain was still there with them, Murcer led the comeback starting with a three-run homer in the seventh off the Orioles Dennis Martinez, which narrowed the gap to one. It was a significant home run for Murcer because it was his first since being reacquired in June and his first at the stadium since 1973. The game went to the bottom of the ninth with the Yanks trailing 4–3. Bucky Dent began the inning with a walk off of Orioles reliever Tippy Martinez. Willie Randolph laid down a sacrifice bunt, but Martinez threw the ball away, putting runners at second and third with no outs.

After delivering the eulogy earlier that day, Murcer delivered a two-run single to left on an 0–2 pitch to give the Yankees a thrilling and emotional 5–4 win. Afterward Murcer said, "Everybody was so tired. I think we were playing on the spirit of Thurman. There was a feeling amongst both teams that somehow Munson was watching. That's what carried us through the game," said the 33-year-old outfielder.

The longest day in Yankees history was over. The team could finally exhale and move forward from this tragic event. The Yankees played out the schedule, but no one, not even their owner George Steinbrenner, cared much that the team would not play in their third straight World Series.

It was time to start healing the wounds and it would take time. "It was gradual, but there were flashbacks," said Kaat.

After that emotional win, the Yankees still found themselves 14 games behind the front-running Orioles. The season was, for all purposes, over. The two-time defending champions did not go down lightly as they fashioned an eight-game winning streak to close the season with an 89–71 record.

The Captain's death would be felt for years to come as the Yankees desperately tried to make up for the loss of Munson's leadership. Because his career was cut short, Munson's candidacy as a Hall of Famer was curtailed as well, but those who watched him play know the value of what he brought to the team on and off the field.

Even today, Munson's locker stands on its own in the Yankees clubhouse. A little plate resides in the middle of the overhang with his No. 15 on it.

Note: The Yankees lost another player on October 11, 2006, when pitcher Cory Lidle was killed in a plane crash on the Upper East Side of New York City.

The Other M&M Boys: Two Great Yankees Who Never Grabbed the Ring

Mel Stottlemyre and Don Mattingly will always hold a place in franchise history as two great Yankees who never played on a world championship team.

The links between the two include the fact that they both played their entire career in pinstripes, both played in only one postseason series, both excelled in their lone appearance, and both lost their series in a deciding game on the road. There was another connection between the two. One came up at the end of a dynasty and the other retired at the beginning of another.

Stottlemyre

Mel Stottlemyre will always hold a place in Yankees lore as a star pitcher who was in the right place, but at the wrong time. Stottlemyre did his best work from 1965 to 1973 when he captured 149 of his 164 career wins, but the Yankees weren't winning championships, so many of his accomplishments went relatively unnoticed. The 6'2" sinker-balling right-hander caught the final chapter of the Yankees dynasty in August 1964. The Bombers were in a dogfight with the Baltimore Orioles and Chicago White Sox for the American League pennant that season.

On August 11, the young pitcher was recalled from Richmond, where he posted a sparkling 1.42 ERA, and the next day he made a stunning major league debut at Yankee Stadium. In his first game, Stottlemyre tossed a complete-game win for the Yankees over the White Sox.

His second start was almost as good, as he pitched eight and two-thirds innings against another contender in Baltimore, giving up a run on five hits. Stottlemyre provided a much-needed shot in the arm as he went 9–3 with a 2.06 ERA down the stretch.

In the 1964 World Series, Stottlemyre beat Hall of Famer Bob Gibson in Game 2 by tossing a complete-game victory. Yankees great Whitey Ford was injured so manager Yogi Berra wanted to ride the young stud by bringing him back for Game 5 on three days rest.

In another matchup with Gibson, Stottlemyre held the Yankees in it, giving up two runs (one earned). That allowed Tom Tresh to tie the game in the ninth with a two-run homer, but the Cards won the game in 10 innings on a three-run homer by Tim McCarver. In Game 7 the two matched up once again, both going with only two days rest.

Mel Stottlemyre (far left) won nearly 200 games for some less-than-competitive Yankees teams during the 1960s and 1970s, but he later tasted championship glory as Manager Joe Torre's (second from left) pitching coach. Bench coach Joe Girardi (second from right) and an unidentified player stand with Stottlemyre and Torre.

TOP 10

All-Time Strikeouts

1.	Whitey Ford	1,956
2.	Ron Guidry	1,778
3.	Red Ruffing	1,526
4.	Lefty Gomez	1,468
5.	Andy Pettitte	1,275
6.	Mel Stottlemyre	1,257
7.	Bob Shawkey	1,163
8.	Al Downing	1,028
9.	Allie Reynolds	967
10.	Roger Clemens	946

The Cardinals Hall of Fame right-hander was up to the task, but Stottlemyre could only go four innings, giving up three runs on five hits as the Yanks lost to St. Louis in seven games.

It was 1965 when the Missouri-born righty posted his first 20-win season, leading the league in complete games with 18 and innings pitched with 291.

Stottlemyre was well known for his nasty sinker and impeccable control. In nine seasons of tossing more than 250 innings, Stottlemyre never walked more than 100 batters.

Mel was more than capable of helping himself at the plate. Late in 1964, Stottlemyre had a five-hit game in Washington against the Senators. A year later, he would hit an inside-the-park grand-slam home run at Yankee Stadium.

The 1966 season was a complete turnaround from 1965 as Stottlemyre became one of a handful of pitchers to win 20 games in one season and lose 20 the next, going 12–20 for the last place Yankees, who won all of 70 games.

In 1967, Mel rebounded to win 15 games and then won 20 in each of the next two seasons.

From 1971 to 1973, Stottlemyre won 46 games, but in 1974 he developed a rotator cuff problem. His career ended following a dismal 6–7 record in 1974. In his 11-year career in pinstripes, Stottlemyre won 164 games and lost 139 with a career ERA of 2.97.

Mattingly

On September 8, 1982, the Yankees beat the Baltimore Orioles at Yankee Stadium 10–5 behind the strong pitching of Jay Howell. It was a fairly meaningless game except for one thing. The game marked the major league debut of Donald Arthur Mattingly. The beloved Yankee would replace Ken Griffey Sr. for defense in left field, his first taste of the bigs. Three days later, he had his first big league at-bat, a foul out to third against Milwaukee's Jim Slaton.

On October 1, against Boston at the stadium, Mattingly stroked his first hit, an eleventh-inning single off the Red Sox Steve Crawford.

After Mattingly began the 1983 season with the big club, he was sent back to Columbus for a short time. Bobby Murcer's retirement opened a roster spot for Mattingly, who was recalled to play first base for the injured Griffey. On June 21 Mattingly started at first and went two for four against Baltimore.

Don Mattingly was the 1985 AL MVP after batting .324 with 35 homers and 145 RBIs.

TOP 10

All-Time Pitching Victories

1.	Whitey Ford	236
2.	Red Ruffing	231
3.	Lefty Gomez	189
4.	Ron Guidry	170
5.	Bob Shawkey	168
6.	Mel Stottlemyre	164
7.	Herb Pennock	162
8.	Waite Hoyt	157
9.	Andy Pettitte	149
10.	Allie Reynolds	131

Mattingly played 91 games and batted .283 for his first real season, but he had not yet accumulated the power numbers that would propel him to be labeled one of the best players in the game for a period of the 1980s.

The breakout season came in 1984. The team struggled early because of a lack of offense, but you couldn't blame Mattingly, who was en route to the batting title. The power numbers surfaced for the first time as the Indiana native's ledger read 23 home runs and 110 runs batted in.

Mattingly was on his way. In 1985 he had a career year that was magnificent. A batting average of .324 with career marks of 35 home runs and 145 RBIs, not to mention 48 doubles among his 211 hits. The numbers added up to a Most Valuable Player award for the young first baseman, the first Yankee to win the coveted honor since Thurman Munson in 1976.

Mattingly's season took on a magical light the night of May 13 when he slammed a walk-off three-run homer to rally the Yankees from an 8–0 deficit and beat Minnesota 9–8. The Yankees surprisingly found themselves in a pennant race with Toronto, and Mattingly was thriving on the big stage.

The Yankees met the Blue Jays for a pivotal four-game set at Yankee Stadium beginning on September 12. The Bombers won the first game but lost the next three to find themselves four and a half games behind the Jays with three weeks left. The team needed a boost, and Mattingly was determined to provide one. In the final 19 games, Mattingly was 26 for 80 with seven home runs and 20 RBIs to help the Yankees take the divisional race down to the final weekend.

Mattingly would total a career high and Yankees record of 238 hits to finish at a sizzling .352 in 1986, but he would come up short to Wade Boggs's .357 in the race for a second batting crown. Mattingly was heading toward greatness with his increased power numbers, but the 1987 season would be the coup de grâce. On July 18, in a game at Arlington Stadium, Mattingly tied Dale Long's all-time record by homering in his eighth straight game. The historic blow came in the top of the fourth off Texas Rangers pitcher Jose Guzman, and it was a drive to the opposite field that cleared the left-field fence.

That wasn't the only home-run achievement of the year for the Yankees first baseman. Late in the season, Mattingly hit a grand-slam home run off Boston's Bruce Hurst at Yankee Stadium, which just happened to be his sixth of the year to set a major league record for a single season. Mattingly finished the season hitting .327 with 30 home runs and 115 RBIs.

After the 1987 campaign, Mattingly's numbers began to decline. He was having trouble with his back, and it was affecting his game. The power numbers dropped first. In 1988 he went from 30 home runs to 18 round-trippers. In 1989 he put it together one more time for a 23 home run, 113 RBI season (his final 100 RBI season) while batting .303.

During his peak years, he averaged more than 26 home runs per season, while in his last four seasons (1992–1995) he averaged 11 home runs per year.

Mattingly was getting very frustrated as his numbers dropped—and the team wasn't exactly winning a lot of games. In what was to be his final season, 1995, Mattingly hit only seven homers, but he got some key hits to help the Yankees secure their first American League wild-card berth. After all the disappointment, Mattingly was finally headed to postseason play, but it would be bittersweet.

TRIVIA

Name the player who was the first Yankee to wear No. 1.

Answers to the trivia questions are on pages 186–187.

The former American League Most Valuable Player acquitted himself very well as he batted .417 with a homer and six RBIs during the ALD race versus Seattle.

In the epic Game 2, Mattingly connected for his only postseason home run as he went back to back with Ruben Sierra to give the Yanks a 3–2 lead before Jim Leyritz ended it in the bottom of the fifteenth with a walk-off two-run blow.

The sellout crowd gave Mattingly an ovation as has rarely been seen. In a funny way, the fans knew that Game 2 would be Mattingly's final home game.

Game 5 turned out to be Mattingly's swan song, but he went out in style. With the score tied at two, Mattingly gave the Yankees the lead with a two-run double that would've served as the winning hit had the Bombers been able to hold on. The Yankees eventually led the game 5–4 in the eleventh with three outs to go—but it wasn't meant to be.

Helpless to do anything about his fate, Mattingly watched Ken Griffey Jr. score all the way from first on Edgar Martinez's two-run double to give Seattle a walk-off Series win and a crushing defeat for the Yankees.

Afterward, Mattingly reflected on what had just occurred. "The experience was great," said the former MVP. "It was a couple of teams who were like warriors out there. Nobody wanted to give in."

Mattingly never announced that he intended to retire, but speculation was rampant that he had played his last game as a Yankee. The Yankees certainly believed that because they went out and acquired first baseman Tino Martinez from Seattle as part of a five-player trade.

Mattingly did something that became a rarity in modern times—he played his entire career with one team. He batted .307 with 222 career home runs. On August 31, 1997, the Yankees retired Donnie Baseball's No. 23.

The Core

During their second championship drought of 1982 to 1995, the Yankees developed a reputation as a team that would buy their players through free agency, while not adding any new parts from what became a barren farm system. That formula never helped the Yankees reach the promised land, and they paid for it with dismal seasons and no apparent future prospects with which to begin the 1990s.

Starting with a switch-hitting center fielder in 1991, the Yankees brought up a core of homegrown talent that made an enormous impact on their latest championship run.

Bernie Williams: The Next Great Center Fielder

When the Yankees promoted 22-year-old switch-hitting center fielder Bernie Williams from the minors in the early 1990s, they didn't expect to have another Mickey Mantle on their hands—but they knew they had something.

The shy, introverted Williams was signed as a 17-year-old, non-drafted free agent in September 1985 and began his professional career at Sarasota of the Gulf Coast League.

The Puerto Rican–born outfielder moved his way up through the Yankees system until he was called to the majors in July 1991 to make his debut against Baltimore.

During the early stages of Williams's career, the Yankees felt he was too soft, too nice to deal with the trials and tribulations that a player has to go through in the transition to the big leagues.

But Williams had an ally in Yankees manager Buck Showalter, who had coached the switch-hitter in the minors. Under Showalter's tutelage, Williams began to blossom as a big league star. Williams hit

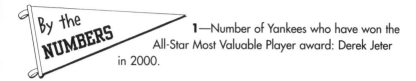

By the NUMBERS

1—Number of Yankees who have won the All-Star Most Valuable Player award: Derek Jeter in 2000.

.268 in 1993, his first full year, but he raised his average to .289 with 12 home runs and 57 RBIs in the 1994 season, which was cut short by a labor dispute.

Nineteen ninety-five saw the Yankees qualify for the playoffs for the first time in 14 years as Williams had a breakout campaign, hitting .307 with 18 home runs and 82 runs batted in.

In the ALDS loss to Seattle, Williams became the first player in history to hit a home run from both sides of the plate in one post-season game and ended up with a .429 average in the series.

Nineteen ninety-six brought more achievements. A .305 average, not to mention a career high in home runs with 29 (the most by a Yankees center fielder since Bobby Murcer slammed 33 in 1972) and runs batted in with 102. One of the highlights of Williams's season was an eight RBI game in Detroit, which included a grand slam and a three-run homer.

With the Yankees advancing to the American League Championship Series for the first time in 15 years, Williams lived up to his potential as he became the second Yankee to win the American League Championship Series Most Valuable Player award. (Graig Nettles was the first in 1981.)

Williams hit .474 against Baltimore including an eleventh-inning, walk-off home run against Orioles reliever Randy Myers to win Game 1 and send the Yankees on their way to the World Series.

The 1997 season brought his first All-Star berth and his first Gold Glove.

The switch-hitting center fielder faced his "walk" year in 1998, and he made it one to remember. The likeable Yankee became the first player to ever win the league batting title, a Gold Glove, and a World Series championship in the same season. His .339 average clinched the batting crown while he took home his second Gold Glove and his second ring.

The clinching game in San Diego was bittersweet because it almost was the final time that Williams would appear in a Yankees uniform. In December 1998, Williams nearly signed with the rival Red Sox, but had a change of heart at the last minute to re-sign with the Bombers. Four more years of a .300 or better batting average and two more World Series wins to total four puts Williams in the elite category of Yankees center fielders. His performance on the field notwithstanding, Williams has exhibited the kind of dignity and class that graced the Yankees pinstripes in the past.

Yankees manager Joe Torre called Williams "the most elegant player I've ever managed." "I never met Arthur Ashe," Torre said, "but I put Bernie right in that category as a person of class."

Going into 2006, Williams was ranked in the Yankees top 10 in seven offensive categories, including home runs and RBIs.

Andy Pettitte: A Second Helping of Lightning from Louisiana

In July 1975, the Yankees debuted a rail-thin left-hander from Lafayette, Louisiana, in the second game of a doubleheader loss to Boston. At the time, no one had heard of Ron Guidry. Going into the spring of 1995, the Yankees brought in a rail-thin left-hander from Baton Rouge, Louisiana. At the time, no one had heard of Andy Pettitte. The 6'5" lefty made his major league debut on April 29, when he was used in relief against the Royals in Kansas City.

After being sent back to the minors for a short stint, Pettitte was called up for good on May 27 and made his first major league start that very day against Oakland where he pitched five and one-third innings but came up on the short end of a 3–0 score. The young southpaw stayed in the rotation for the remainder of the year and went on to a 12–9 record. He was paying dividends down the stretch of the 1995 season. Pettitte became the fifth Yankees rookie starter to win five games after September 1 as he went 5–1 and helped the Bombers qualify for the American League's first wild-card berth. Pettitte had the most wins by a rookie and finished third in the American League's Rookie of the Year voting.

The Yankees left-hander took his game to another level in 1996 as he won 21 games for the World Series champions, including a huge Game 5 victory in the World Series against Atlanta. Pettitte got the nod for Game 1 but was hammered. In two and one-third innings, the southpaw gave up seven runs. He would be redeemed just four days later in the final game ever played at Atlanta's Fulton County Stadium. The lefty went "toe to toe" with Braves starter John Smoltz, whose only blemish was an unearned run. Behind Pettitte, the Yanks took a 1–0 decision. The lefty had his first World Series win, and the Yankees had a 3–2 lead in the Series after being down 2–0.

One big advantage Pettitte brought with him to the big leagues was an incredibly deceptive pickoff move to first base. In his first full season, the tall left-hander picked off 12 runners at first while making opposing runners wary of taking leads whenever he was on the mound. Pettitte began the 1997 campaign with a 5–0 mark and went on to win 18 games while posting a 2.88 earned-run average.

On September 5 Pettitte was drilled in the face by a Cal Ripken line drive and suffered contusions of the left thumb and lip, along with a small laceration on the nose. Eleven days later, he tossed eight shutout innings against Boston and struck out a career-high 12 batters in a 2–0 win.

Pettitte continued to pile up impressive numbers during the Yankees magical season of 1998. After a slow start, the Louisiana-born lefty rebounded to win 16 games. Pettitte's season was capped off by a Game 4 victory at San Diego to wrap up the Yanks second consecutive World Series championship and 24th title overall. The 22nd-round pick in the June 1990 draft tossed seven and one-third scoreless innings in winning his second World Series game.

The 1999 and 2000 seasons produced a total of 33 more wins and two more World Series championships, including a start in the Series-clinching Game 5 against the Mets. Pettitte did not get the win but he tossed seven innings and gave up two runs, both unearned, to keep the Yanks in it.

The big lefty continued to maintain his consistency winning 15 games in 2001 and 13 in 2002, as he became the first pitcher in the post-expansion era (after 1961) to win at least 12 games in each of his first eight seasons.

In his final Yankees season (2003), Pettitte won a career-high-tying 21 games. Overall, in Pettitte's starts, the Yankees were 23–10, and that success carried over to the postseason in a big way. During the 2003 playoffs, the Yankees had a penchant for losing the first game and then relying on Andy Pettitte to bail them out in Game 2.

The Yankees were already down a game to the Minnesota Twins in the opening round best-of-five series, so winning Game 2 was an absolute must. Pettitte gave the Yanks just what they needed. Seven solid innings, where he gave up a run on three hits while striking out 10 in earning a huge 4–1 win.

The Yanks advanced to the league championship series for a best-of-seven with Boston and lost the opening game at Yankee Stadium.

It was Pettitte to the rescue once again as he got the win with seven innings of two-run ball in a series-evening 6–2 victory in Game 2.

Finally in the World Series against Florida, the Bombers lost the opener and Pettitte was in position for Game 2. He did not disappoint as he nearly became the first Yankees pitcher in 25 years (since Jim Beattie in Game 5 of the 1978 Series) to go the distance in a Series game.

Pettitte had a four-hit shutout going to the ninth and got to within one out of becoming the first Yankees pitcher to toss a complete game shutout (the first since Ralph Terry shut out the Giants in Game 7 of the 1962 Series). But an error by third baseman Aaron Boone allowed Florida to score an unearned run, and the left-hander left the game with two out in the ninth.

Mo, the Closer

During the Yankees' run of three-straight World Series victories from 1998 to 2000, a familiar sight on the mound at the end of the clinching game was (if you can imagine the great Bob Sheppard saying it) "numburr for-tee-too, Mahr-ree-ahn-oh Ree-veh-ra, numburr for-tee-too."

Just as Sparky Lyle had "Pomp and Circumstance" to announce his entrance into the game, Rivera has Metallica's "Enter Sandman" to usher him in. As soon as the first few notes of the heavy-metal classic are heard, the crowd responds because they know it's time for Mo (as he's affectionately referred to by his teammates).

The Panama-born Rivera made his way through the Yankees farm system with one blip on the radar screen. In August 1992 Rivera underwent surgery on his right elbow so his status as a top Yankees prospect waned a bit. After a year at Class A Greensboro and Tampa, Rivera went to Columbus (at the end of the 1994 season).

On May 16, 1995, Rivera was called up for the first time and made his big-league debut on May 23, when he started and gave up five runs on eight hits in three and one-third innings pitched in a 10–0 loss to the Angels in Anaheim.

Rivera got his first major-league win against Oakland on May 28, but his next two starts at Yankee Stadium were nothing to write home about, so he was sent back to Columbus on June 11. He was recalled on July 4, and that night in Chicago he dazzled the White Sox with eight innings of shutout ball where he struck out a career-high 11 batters.

Rivera made his first big-league relief appearance in Milwaukee where he blew a save opportunity but got the win in a 7–5 Yankees victory.

On September 1 a peek at Rivera's future greatness was revealed when Rivera tossed three and two-thirds innings of one-run relief to set up John Wetteland for the save in a big 8–7 Yankees win. The Yankees found themselves in the race for the first-ever American League wild-card berth, and Rivera was becoming a big part of their success.

Four days later, Rivera started for the final time, but he got hit around in a game against Seattle. After that he began his illustrious career in the bullpen.

Rivera finished out the 1995 season with six more appearances out of the pen, including an out in the wild-card clincher on the final day of the 1995 season.

The Panamanian dynamo made his mark in the postseason in Game 2 of the division series race against Seattle. It was an epic battle in which Rivera earned the win by tossing the final three and one-third innings, giving up no runs on two hits with five strikeouts.

Jim Leyritz's walk-off home run in the fifteenth was the story line that night, but Rivera was just beginning to carve his way into Yankees lore.

In 1996 Rivera combined with Wetteland to form the most potent one-two combination the Yankees had ever had out of their bullpen. The duo was "lights out" in almost every appearance, and they provided Manager Joe Torre and the Yankees a comfort zone that gave them the confidence to know that if they had a late-inning lead, the game was theirs.

On May 17 Rivera earned his first major league save against the Angels when he closed an 8–5 win for Andy Pettitte. The success continued right through the postseason that led to the club's 23rd World Series championship and Rivera's first with more to come. Rivera made eight appearances in the postseason and gave up a total of one run.

Mariano Rivera continues to add to his résumé as one of the most dominant closers of all time.

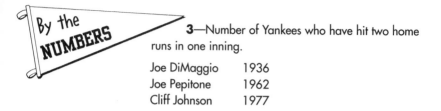

3—Number of Yankees who have hit two home runs in one inning.

Joe DiMaggio	1936
Joe Pepitone	1962
Cliff Johnson	1977

Wetteland left the Yanks after the Series to sign with the Texas Rangers as a free agent, and "Mo" was ready to step in as the full-time closer.

Rivera got his first two saves on the road and had a chance to close out a 1–0 home-opening win on April 11 versus Oakland, but Mark McGwire gave the Yanks an omen of things to come that season when he homered off Rivera in the ninth to tie a game the Bombers would go on to lose.

Rivera tied Wetteland for second place on the Yanks all-time, single-season save list with 43—but in the division series playoff against Cleveland, disaster struck. The Yankees were prepared to close out the Indians in Game 4 at Jacobs Field, but Rivera gave up a game-tying home run to Sandy Alomar Jr., and Cleveland rallied to take Game 4 and the series in Game 5.

"The first and only time I saw him rattled was the 1997 season," said Torre. "He's got ice water in his veins."

A motivated Yankees team took the field in 1998 for a record 125 total wins and a second World Series championship in three years.

Rivera saved 36 games in the regular season and then six more in the postseason. In total, Rivera made 10 postseason appearances, including all four games in the World Series, and he did not give up a run.

Nineteen ninety-nine was even better as the 29-year-old converted on 45 of 49 save opportunities. Rivera's numbers from 1999 are absolutely astounding. He retired 60 of 66 first batters he faced, and he did not allow a run in his final 28 appearances of the season. He converted his last 22 save opportunities, gave up only two home runs all year, (Detroit's Bobby Higginson and Atlanta's Andruw Jones) and also prevented 22 of 27 inherited runners from scoring.

"Nobody better," said his admiring manager. "He's one of the few you can bring in for a non-save situation, and he will give you the same exact focus it takes to get the job done."

Another strong postseason for the right-hander with 12⅓ scoreless innings in eight games, including a win and two saves in the four-game World Series sweep of Atlanta, where he became only the third reliever to win the Series Most Valuable Player award.

The year 2000 saw the Yankees win their third-straight title. For the third year in a row Rivera was on the mound for the final out of the Series as the Mets' Mike Piazza flew out to left-center field to give the Yankees a World Series victory over their crosstown rivals.

It seemed like nothing could stop Rivera as the Yankees rallied in 2001 to defeat Oakland in the division series race and Seattle for the pennant.

In the World Series against Arizona, the Yankees had a 2–1 lead in the bottom of the ninth inning of Game 7. This time, Rivera faltered. Arizona's Mark Grace led off the inning with a single, and then Rivera made a key throwing error at second to set up the crushing rally.

After a force out at third, Tony Womack doubled in the tying run with the winning run going to third. Craig Counsell was hit by a pitch to load the bases. With the infield in, Luis Gonzalez lifted a bloop single past Derek Jeter at short, and the Yankees championship run was over. Despite a Yankees record-setting season with 50 saves, Rivera suffered an ink stain on what otherwise was an unblemished résumé. It was the first time since 1997 that he had blown a postseason save. Quite a stretch of success, but it proved all along that Rivera was human.

Despite that devastating defeat, Rivera earned the title of greatest closer of all time. He's headed to the Hall of Fame. It's just that he's not done compiling records yet.

Derek Jeter: Captain

In June 1992, the Yankees traveled an unfamiliar road to plant a seed that sprouted into a championship run to rival the great Bomber teams of past years. The Yankees had the sixth overall pick in the 1992 draft, and they chose a skinny, 17-year-old, 6'3", 175-pound shortstop from Kalamazoo Central High School named Derek Sanderson Jeter.

For the most part, the Yankees had been less than successful with first-round picks. Up until 1992, the most notable first rounder was Thurman Munson, who was chosen fourth overall in the 1968 draft.

The kid from Kalamazoo moved rapidly through the Yankees farm system. By the end of the 1994 season, Jeter had worked his way to Columbus where he hit .349 with 44 hits in 35 games. Jeter's propensity for winning was already being felt. In 1994 the Yankees minor league affiliates played at a .621 winning percentage with Jeter on their roster. Without him, the percentage dropped to .502. Yankees general manager Gene Michael could not have been more pleased with his first-round selection. "He's the real thing," said Michael. "I liked what I saw of him. He's getting there."

Nineteen ninety-five saw the first-round pick play most of the season with Columbus, but he got his first taste of major league baseball when he was called up on May 29. The New Jersey–born Jeter, who grew up rooting for the Yankees and idolizing Dave Winfield, was ready for his first taste of the bigs. Jeter went 0 for 5 in his first game, but the next day he got his first major league hit, a single off Tim Belcher.

In 1996 Derek Jeter became the Yankees' first rookie to start at shortstop since 1962. Photo courtesy of Albert Coqueran.

The Yanks sent their prized prospect back to Columbus in early June and then called him back in September for a brief two-game stint. It was the last time Jeter saw the minor leagues.

In 1996 Jeter became the first rookie shortstop (since Tom Tresh in 1962) to start for the Yankees, and he didn't disappoint as he put together an outstanding first season. Yankees manager Joe Torre had never seen the youngster play but had heard only good things. Torre said, "The organization feels it's his time to play."

Jeter relished the challenge. "I'm going to be ready to earn the job," he said.

Torre said, "He had that look in his eyes. He had leadership qualities from the first day I met him." It began on Opening Day in Cleveland when the 21-year-old connected for his first big league home run off Indians pitcher Dennis Martinez. Jeter also made a great defensive play as he roamed into the outfield to catch a pop-up with an over-the-shoulder grab.

There was magic in the air in 1996. Jeter had his first four-hit game, which included a tie-breaking, two-run single in the seventh inning of a 7–5 win over Boston in July. The Yankees went on to capture the division title and Jeter carried his terrific regular season right into the postseason where he hit .361.

Dave Anderson, the award-winning sportswriter for *The New York Times,* wrote, "The kid at shortstop has been the difference in their season."

Jeter's reputation for being a big-game player originated with the 1996 postseason. In Game 2 against Texas in the divisional playoffs, Jeter scored the game-winning run in the bottom of the twelfth on a throwing error by Rangers third baseman Dean Palmer.

In the American League Championship Series, he hit a controversial home run in Game 1 where a fan (Jeffrey Maier) reached out over the wall to interfere with Orioles right fielder Tony Tarasco. Maier caught the ball while reaching over the wall, but right field line umpire Rich Garcia called a home run.

The series ended in storybook fashion as future Hall of Famer Cal Ripken grounded to the young star who threw him out, and the Yankees wrapped up their first American League pennant since 1981.

All-Time Yankees Team

Position	Name
Right-Handed Pitcher	Chief Bender
Catcher	Yogi Berra
First Baseman	Lou Gehrig
Second Baseman	Tony Lazzeri
Shortstop	Derek Jeter
Third Baseman	Graig Nettles
Left Fielder	Mickey Mantle
Center Fielder	Joe DiMaggio
Right Fielder	Babe Ruth
Designated Hitter	Don Mattingly
Right-Handed Starter	Red Ruffing
Left-Handed Starter	Whitey Ford
Right-Handed Reliever	Mariano Rivera
Left-Handed Reliever	Sparky Lyle
Manager	Casey Stengel

Second Team

Position	Name
Catcher	Bill Dickey
First Baseman	Bill Skowron
Second Baseman	Joe Gordon
Shortstop	Phil Rizzuto
Third Baseman	Clete Boyer
Left Fielder	Bob Meusel
Center Fielder	Earle Combs
Right Fielder	Roger Maris
Designated Hitter	Reggie Jackson
Right-Handed Starter	Allie Reynolds
Left-Handed Starter	Ron Guidry
Right-Handed Reliever	Goose Gossage
Left-Handed Reliever	Dave Righetti

The Yanks went on to win the Series as Jeter became the fifth freshman in American League history to win the Rookie of the Year Award by a unanimous vote.

Jeter's second full year provided his first taste of defeat. After his average dropped 23 points to .291, Jeter rebounded in the division playoffs against Cleveland to hit a sparkling .333 with two home runs and six runs scored.

It wasn't enough as the Indians rallied to beat the Yankees in five games. The lasting picture from that defeat was one of Jeter staring out onto the field, watching the Indians celebrate. That moment served to motivate the Yankees shortstop for the 1998 season.

The Yankees plowed through the regular season like a runaway train, winning a record 114 games. Jeter's contribution was a .324 average with 19 home runs and 84 RBIs, not to mention 203 hits and 127 runs scored. The pressure was on the Yankees to go all the way or their regular-season heroics would be all for naught.

The Yankees swept Texas in the division, but they struggled with Cleveland in the ALCS. The Yankees rallied to take a 3–2 series lead and then led Game 6 6–5 after blowing a 6–0 lead. With runners at first and second and one out in the sixth, Jeter lined a triple to right field to score two more and increase the Yankee lead to 8–5.

The Bombers would go on to a 9–5, pennant-clinching win followed by a four-game sweep of San Diego in the World Series.

Nineteen ninety-nine became Jeter's signature season as he put it all together to post a .349 average with 24 home runs and 102 RBIs. The former first-round draft pick had a career high of 219 hits and 91 walks.

The Yankees won the pennant and then took home back-to-back titles for the first time since the late 1970s following a four-game sweep of the Braves in the final Series of the century. Jeter hit .353 in the Series and captured his third championship ring in four years.

The Yankees were looking to become the first team since the Oakland A's of the 1970s to win three consecutive World Series championships.

Jeter put together another solid season where he captured the MVP of the All-Star Game, but it was the 2000 World Series against the New York Mets where the Yankees shortstop got to shine again on the big stage.

Jeter took home Most Valuable Player after the Yankees beat their crosstown rivals in five games to win their third championship in a row.

After the Mets had taken Game 3 at Shea Stadium and appeared to have some momentum, Jeter stole it right back by leading off Game 4 with a home run that set the tone for the remainder of the series.

The MVP was 9 for 22 (.409), with two home runs, two RBIs, and six runs scored, but it was his timing and flair for the dramatic that were on display. Jeter is a born leader and one who is writing his own piece of Yankees history.

Jorge Posada: Geor-gee

Names like Butch Wynegar and Dioner Navarro have worn the pin-stripes as switch-hitting Yankees catchers, but the best switch-hitting backstop the Yanks have ever had is named Jorge Posada. Posada came from major league stock. His uncle, Leo, was a major league outfielder in the 1960s for the Kansas City Athletics.

The Puerto Rican native was drafted in 1990 as a second baseman and played one year at that position for Oneonta in the A league. It was decided that Posada would be better served as a catcher, and he made the transition in 1992 when he caught for Greensboro of Class A.

In 1993 Posada split the season between Prince William and Albany. It was becoming apparent that the switch-hitter was going to provide some power from that position after he hit 17 home runs.

After an injury-plagued season in 1994 at Columbus (a home-plate collision cut short his campaign), Posada was called up to the big club in 1995 for a "cup of coffee." "Georgie" became a pinch runner in Game 2 of the division series loss to Seattle and actually scored the tying run that sent the game to its eventual conclusion in 15 innings.

Posada was the club's future at catcher, but in the interim the Yankees acquired veteran backstop Joe Girardi to be the starter in

1996. Girardi played a role in Posada's development by lending advice and counsel to the young switch-hitter.

In 1997 Posada really got his feet wet by appearing in 60 games. Nineteen ninety-eight was his breakout year as he played in 111 games, hitting 17 homers with 63 RBIs. After Girardi signed with the Chicago Cubs as a free agent, Posada became the number-one backstop.

Posada's numbers actually fell in 1999, but 2000 proved to be a productive season for Posada who hit 28 home runs and drove home 86. Posada played in 151 games as the Yankees captured their third-straight title. Going for four in a row, Posada made a huge contribution in the third game of the 2001 division series against Oakland. First, the switch-hitting backstop hit a home run off A's left-hander Barry Zito that proved to be the only run of the game. Second, Posada was on the receiving end of Derek Jeter's famous flip play to nail Oakland's Jeremy Giambi at the plate.

The nephew of Leo Posada has been on the receiving end of some great Yankees moments throughout his career. In 1998 Posada caught David Wells's perfect game and, in 2003, he backstopped Roger Clemens's 300th career win.

Posada's career year came in 2003 as he hit .281 with 30 home runs and 101 RBIs. He topped it off with the biggest hit of the Game 7 epic against Boston. With runners at second and third and one out in the eighth inning, the Yankees trailed 5–3 against Pedro Martinez when Posada's bloop double into short center field tied the game. Aaron Boone became the hero later that night, but without Posada's clutch hit, Boone may never have gotten his golden opportunity.

In his Yankees career, Jorge Posada has homered from both sides of the plate five times.

Posada's defense has been questioned at times, but Joe Torre is very fond of his catcher. "I love him like a son," Torre said. "He's passionate about the game."

These five farm products combined for a total of 20 championship rings. The Yankees are hoping to reap some more benefits in the very near future.

1995 Season: They're Back!

The year was 1994, and the Yankees thought it was their year. New York had the best record in the American League on August 12 when the players went on strike. The remainder of the regular season and the entire postseason was cancelled. The Yankees could only ponder what could have been. "I thought we were getting ready to go on a big-time run," said Yankees manager Buck Showalter.

Fourteen years had passed since the Yankees last tasted a postseason berth, so they felt good about their chances going into 1995, but there was still the matter of the labor dispute. The players and owners finally settled their differences in March 1995, and the season began in late April.

The Yankees started off with a 10–5 mark, but they dropped 14 of their next 17 to stand at 13–19. Nineteen ninety-five was the first year that the wild-card playoff team would be added to the postseason menu, so there was more at stake than just the division crown.

Showalter tried to put a positive spin on the slide that left his club in last place, eight and a half games behind Boston in the American League East. "Teams go through situations like this," said Showalter, "but we've got to work through it. There are no magical answers."

By the All-Star break, the Yankees were 30–36, the season being shortened because of the labor strife. There was a feeling that this slow start was due to a "hangover" from 1994. The Yankees were eight games back and needed a strong second half if they had aspirations of qualifying for the postseason.

A seven-game winning streak in late July helped the Yankees back to .500, but they continued to stumble, and on August 26 they were 53–58, 15½ games behind the Red Sox. One big consideration was that the Yankees, despite being five under .500, were in second place, which meant they were right in the thick of the wild-card race. The club took this cue and ran with it, taking 13 of their next 16 games to go to 66–61, one-half game up in the wild-card race with 17 left to play.

After a frustrating shutout loss to Kevin Brown and the Orioles, the Yankees were 68–64, one game behind Seattle for the wild-card lead—but the Texas Rangers climbed into a flat-footed tie with New York. Twelve games to go, and it was certainly crunch time. "They're all big," said Yankees pitcher Scott Kamieniecki.

The Yankees began the "do or die" stretch of their season in style as they ran off a six-game winning streak. One of those wins was a come-from-behind victory against Toronto where they trailed 4–0 but rallied for a five-run eighth to score an important 6–4 win. Ruben Sierra's three-run homer was the key blow, and the win left the Bombers a half game behind Seattle and the California Angels, who were tied for first in the AL West, along with the wild-card standings.

The Yankees completed their home season by having the six-game winning streak snapped by Detroit. It wasn't a crushing loss; the Yanks still led the Angels by a half game with five games left, all on the road.

First up, a two-game series in Milwaukee where the Yankees always had problems winning. Earlier in the year, the Yankees had dropped two of three at County Stadium. The opener was a nail biter that came down to the final at-bat.

Yankees closer John Wetteland was able to get the final four outs to secure a big win, while rookie Derek Jeter, who started at shortstop so that Randy Velarde could play the outfield in place of Bernie Williams, doubled home an important run with his first and only at-bat.

IF ONLY . . . Tony Kubek had not gotten hit in the Adam's apple by Bill Virdon's bad-hop single in Game 7 of the 1960 World Series. Many pointed to that play as the turning point of the Series because that could have produced one out and maybe two. The Pirates went on to score five runs to take a 9–7 lead before the Yankees tied it to set up Bill Mazeroski's heroics.

By the NUMBERS

20—Number of postseason walk-off wins by the Yankees

October 8, 1927: Yanks 4, Pirates 3 (Game 4 World Series)
Yanks win on walk-off wild pitch from Pirates' Johnny Miljus

October 4, 1939: Yanks 2, Reds 1 (Game 1 World Series)
Bill Dickey's RBI single off the Reds' Paul Derringer

October 5, 1949: Yanks 2, Dodgers 1 (Game 1 World Series)
Tommy Henrich homers off Brooklyn's Don Newcombe to lead off the ninth

October 6, 1950: Yanks 3, Phillies 2 (Game 3 World Series)
Jerry Coleman's RBI single off the Phillies' Russ Meyer

October 5, 1953: Yanks 4, Dodgers 3 (Game 6 World Series) ** ended series
Billy Martin's RBI single off the Dodgers' Clem Labine

October 10, 1964: Yanks 2, Cardinals 1 (Game 3 World Series)
Mantle hits first pitch of ninth inning from Cards' Barney Schultz for the game winner

October 14, 1976: Yanks 7, Royals 6 (Game 5 ALCS)
Chambliss hits first pitch of ninth inning for famous pennant-winning home run off KC's Mark Littell

October 11, 1977: Yanks 4, Dodgers 3 (Game 1 World Series)
Paul Blair singles off L.A.'s Rick Rhoden to score Randolph in the eleventh

October 14, 1978: Yanks 5, Dodgers 4 (Game 4 World Series)
Lou Piniella singles off L.A.'s Bob Welch to drive in White with game winner

October 4, 1995: Yanks 7, Mariners 5 (Game 2 ALDS)
Jim Leyritz blasts game-winning two-run homer off Seattle's Tim Belcher in fifteenth

October 2, 1996: Yanks 5, Rangers 4 (Game 2 ALDS)
Derek Jeter scores winning run on sacrifice bunt from Hayes and an error on 3B Dean Palmer

October 9, 1996: Yanks 5, Orioles 4 (Game 1 ALCS)
Bernie Williams homers off Baltimore's Randy Myers in twelfth

October 13, 1999: Yanks 4, Red Sox 3 (Game 1 ALCS)
Bernie Williams homers off Boston's Rod Beck in tenth

October 26, 1999: Yanks 5, Braves 4 (Game 3 World Series)
Chad Curtis homers off Atlanta's Mike Remlinger in tenth

October 21, 2000: Yanks 4, Mets 3 (Game 1 World Series)
Jose Vizcaino singles off Mets reliever Turk Wendell to score Tino Martinez in the twelfth

October 21, 2001: Yanks 3, Mariners 1 (Game 3 ALCS)
Alfonso Soriano hits a two-run homer off M's Kaz Sasaki in ninth

October 31, 2001: Yanks 4, Arizona 3 (Game 4 World Series)
Derek Jeter hits walk-off home run in tenth after Martinez ties it in ninth with two-run home run

November 1, 2001: Yanks 3, Arizona 2 (Game 5 World Series)
Soriano singles in game winner in twelfth after Brosius ties it in ninth with a two-run home run

October 16, 2003: Yanks 7, Red Sox 6 (Game 7 ALCS)
Aaron Boone homers off Tim Wakefield on first pitch of the eleventh

October 6, 2004: Yanks 7, Twins 6 (Game 2 ALCS)
Hideki Matsui's sacrifice fly caps a two-run comeback after Minnesota scored in the top of the twelfth and led the series 1–0

Williams was a late arrival from Puerto Rico after he went home to see his brand-new daughter who was born two weeks earlier. Williams missed a flight but was on the field by the third inning, replacing Jeter in the lineup.

The game came down to Wetteland against Milwaukee's David Hulse. The Yankees closer mowed down Hulse with a fastball with two runners on base to end the eighth and pitched a perfect ninth, and the club was a game and a half in front of California, who had lost earlier in the day.

David Cone set the Yankees flying into the final off day of the season as he beat Milwaukee to give the Bombers a two-game sweep. The former Cy Young Award winner was a savior for the Yankees. After he was acquired from Toronto on July 28, Cone posted a 9–2 record. "He has come as advertised," Showalter said.

Following an off day, the Yankees were ready to open the final series of the season, a three-game set in Toronto at Skydome. The first game turned out to be the biggest win of the season. Trailing 3–0 entering the ninth, the Yankees were staring at a record of 0–55 when trailing after eight, but this time they would not go quietly. A key error by the Blue Jays allowed the Yankees to score one run and then a second on a sacrifice fly from Mike Stanley. With a runner on first and one out, Toronto elected to pitch to light-hitting second baseman Pat Kelly. It was Kelly's moment to shine as he stroked a 2–2 pitch for a two-run homer off Toronto reliever Tony Castillo.

"I don't know if it surprised me, but it felt good," said the Yankees hero. "I don't hit too many where I know it's gone."

Wetteland pitched a scoreless ninth for his 31st save, so with two days left, the Yankees had a one-game lead over the Angels for the wild-card spot. Both the Angels and Yankees won on the penultimate day of the season. Going into the final day, the Bombers had control of their own destiny. Win, and they were in.

The Yankees made sure to not let the final game be one of intrigue and mystery. The only question was who would start the game. Showalter knew that the only way he would have a chance at winning a potential five-game playoff was to have Cone start Game 1 and Game 5. With the worst scenario being a one-game playoff for the spot on Monday, Cone would be ready for that game or Game 1 of the division series Tuesday night, so Showalter chose Sterling Hitchcock, who gave the Yanks what they needed.

The Bombers scored twice in the first two innings and never looked back in a 6–1, season-ending win over the Blue Jays that clinched the very first American League wild-card berth.

It was a long and arduous road for Don Mattingly, but it finally paid off with some glory. When Toronto's Randy Knorr grounded into a force play at second for the final out, Mattingly knelt down on one knee and banged his fist into the ground. The long wait, 1,785 games to be exact, was over. Mattingly was headed to the postseason for the first time in his 14-year career. "I am excited inside," said the Yankees first baseman, "but we've still got a lot of work to do." Mattingly's teammates were thrilled to help him reach the playoffs for the first time.

"There is a silent torch that we have all carried for Donnie," said Showalter.

Few knew the pain and turmoil Mattingly went through to be able to play in the final weeks. Showalter told a story of how Mattingly came to him on an airplane flight and said, "Whether my back completely goes or it doesn't, I'm going to let it fly."

"Obviously, it's pretty emotional where Donnie [is] concerned," said Showalter.

The Yankees were back in the postseason, and it began with Game 1 at a raucous Yankee Stadium. New York took the opener, 9–6, behind the pitching of Cone to go along with Wade Boggs and Bernie Williams, who batted one-two in the order and produced a 6 for 10 night with four runs scored and four batted in.

Game 2 was an epic that really helped launch baseball back into the public mainstream. The place was never so loud as when Mattingly

Don Mattingly homers during Game 2 of the 1995 American League divisional series against the Mariners, the only postseason of his great career.

hit his first and only postseason home run, a solo shot off Andy Benes that gave the Yankees a 3–2 lead. The stadium erupted in a stream of jarring noise. "I thought the building was going to come down," said Showalter. "It got so loud we had to resort to using hand signals down to the bullpen because you couldn't hear anything on the phone."

The game was tied at four heading into extra innings. Seattle took a 5–4 lead in the top of the twelfth on a home run from Ken Griffey Jr., but the Yanks tied it in their half on Ruben Sierra's two-out double. On that hit, Bernie Williams was thrown out at the plate for the potential winning run, so the game went on.

In the bottom of the fifteenth, Jim Leyritz hit the first of his two historic Yankees postseason home runs (Leyritz's three-run homer tied Game 4 against Atlanta in the 1996 World Series) when he connected off Tim Belcher for the walk-off winner.

The Yankees needed just one more win to advance to the league championship series for the first time in 14 years. That win never came. The Yankees went on to lose Games 3, 4, and 5, the clincher on a walk-off double by Edgar Martinez in the bottom of the ninth.

It proved to be Don Mattingly's last hurrah.

No-No's: Yankees Pitchers' No-Hitters

Whitey Ford never did it. Neither did Ron Guidry or Red Ruffing. You would figure that in the long and glorious history of the New York Yankees at least one of their all-time great pitchers would have thrown a no-hitter or two.

To throw a no-no, a pitcher needs to have complete command of his pitches sprinkled in with a pinch of luck. The best pitchers in the history of the sport have come up empty in their bids to pitch a no-hit game. The Yankees have had 10 pitchers throw 11 no-hitters, but the most famous pitching performance of all time did not come from one of their all-time greats. Instead it was a journeyman hurler who had complete command of his pitches and a pinch of luck one glorious October afternoon at Yankee Stadium.

October 8, 1956

After trailing two games to none in the 1956 World Series, the Yankees rallied to win Games 3 and 4 at Yankee Stadium. Game 5 would leave the winner needing one of the two remaining games to win the Series while the losers would have their backs against the wall.

Yankees manager Casey Stengel chose a 27-year-old right-handed pitcher named Don Larsen to pitch this pivotal game. The Brooklyn Dodgers went with righty Sal Maglie. "The Barber," as he was affectionately known because he would pitch inside, won 13 games for Brooklyn during the 1956 season and went the distance to win Game 1 of the Series at Ebbets Field.

Larsen won 11 games in 1956 but was the losing pitcher in Game 2 against Brooklyn as he gave up four unearned runs on four hits in one and two-thirds innings pitched.

For a little more than a month, Larsen had been using a no-windup delivery. Despite his failures in Game 2, he stuck with the mechanical adjustment.

Larsen began the game by striking out leadoff hitter Junior Gilliam and the second batter Pee Wee Reese. The strikeout of Reese in the first was notable because it was the only time in the game that Larsen went to a three ball count on any hitter. It was 3–2, and Reese looked at a called third strike from home-plate umpire Babe Pinelli.

Larsen completed the first by getting Duke Snider to line out to right field.

Brooklyn's Jackie Robinson led off the second inning with a hot smash toward third base. The ball caromed off of Yankees third baseman Andy Carey and went right to shortstop Gil McDougald, who threw out the speedy Dodgers third baseman at first.

Both pitchers were in command. So much so that they both set down the first nine hitters they faced.

Larsen went through the first tier of the Dodgers' batting order in the top of the fourth but not without a scare. With two out, Snider lined a ball toward the right-field seats, but it curved foul. Larsen then caught The Duke of Flatbush with a called third strike.

Maglie retired the first two Yankees hitters in the home fourth making it 11 straight set down, but that streak would come to a grinding halt. Mickey Mantle was the hitter, and he fell behind the count, 0–2. Mantle swung at Maglie's next pitch and lined the ball toward the right-field stands. The only question was, fair or foul? This one stayed fair for the first hit of the game and a 1–0 lead.

The Dodgers' fifth opened with Robinson flying out to Hank Bauer in right. The next batter was Gil Hodges, and it turned out to be one of the key at-bats in the game. Hodges drove a pitch toward left-center field for what seemed like a certain hit, but Mantle got a tremendous jump and made a terrific backhanded grab in the gap to preserve the pitching gem.

Dodgers left fielder Sandy Amoros grounded out to second, and Larsen had set down 15 in a row. Thoughts of *could he do it?* began to circulate among the huge crowd of more than 64,000 (which included Yankees-manager-to-be Joe Torre).

Maglie was keeping the Dodgers in the game setting the Yankees down in the fifth, but after the 39-year-old struck out to become Larsen's 18th out, he ran into some trouble in the sixth. Andy Carey began the inning with a single and was sacrificed to second by Larsen. Bauer's one-out single to left scored Carey with the second run.

TRIVIA

Name the former Milwaukee Brewers pitcher who beat the Yankees in the 1981 division series and wore a Yankees uniform in the movie *Major League.*

Answers to the trivia questions are on pages 186–187.

After Joe Collins's single put runners on the corners, Maglie made a big pitch to get Mantle to bounce into a 3–2–5–2–5, inning-ending, double play.

Nine outs to go, but Larsen could not think of greatness. A two-run lead against the Dodgers lineup was far from secure. A ground out and two fly-outs and the Dodgers were gone in the seventh. Twenty-one straight for Larsen. Just six outs away from baseball immortality. After the Yankees went down in their half of the seventh, Larsen took the mound for the eighth.

The anticipation of what was to come could not be measured. For those who were lucky enough to be there that day, or listening to the classic game on the radio, or even watching it on television, it seemed that absolutely everybody—even Dodgers fans—was rooting for the 6'4", 226-pound professional athlete to provide a thrill. Larsen got Robinson on a ground-out to start the inning. Hodges was the next hitter, and he had gotten some good swings against the Yankees right-hander all game long.

The Dodgers first baseman hit a line smash toward third, which was grabbed by Carey for the second out, and Larsen had dodged (no pun intended) a bullet. Amoros flied to center to make it 24 in a row. The legend-to-be led off the bottom of the eighth inning to a thunderous standing ovation from the sellout crowd as he approached the plate.

The most forgiving strikeout in the history of major league baseball was recorded when Larsen went down against Maglie, who was throwing well also, but not good enough.

The tension during the ninth inning was palpable.

Dodgers right fielder Carl Furillo was up first in the ninth and battled Larsen for six pitches until he flied to Bauer in right. Hall of Fame catcher Roy Campanella was next, and on a 0–1 pitch, he grounded weakly to Billy Martin at second base. One out away and a pesky pinch-hitter in Dale Mitchell stood between Larsen and history.

Mitchell batted for Maglie, who pitched a gutsy eight innings, keeping the Dodgers in it. Mitchell was known as a hitter who put his bat on the ball, so it was tough to fool the left-handed swinger.

The first pitch missed high for ball one, but Larsen threw a strike on the second pitch to even the count. Mitchell offered at the next one, but he swung and missed as he fell behind 1–2, and then stayed alive with a foul ball into the left-field stands.

Larsen's final pitch has been captured brilliantly in one classic photo. As Larsen is about to unleash the famous toss, he is seen in his windup with the auxiliary scoreboard in right-center field at Yankee Stadium behind him showing all those zeroes for Brooklyn. All 11 of them (eight innings plus runs, hits, and errors).

One more zero was about to be added to the final line.

Larsen threw the pitch, Yankees catcher Yogi Berra caught it, and the home-plate umpire threw up his right arm to signal strike three.

A moment of baseball history was secure.

Berra trotted out to greet Larsen and jumped on the newest Yankees hero, who grabbed him with both arms. An energized clubhouse could only marvel at the feat.

Manager Casey Stengel used three words to put the achievement in perspective: "Wonderful, just wonderful," said the Old Professor.

Before Larsen's "perfecto" in 1956, the Yankees had four pitchers decorate their record books with no-hit gems.

The first was in 1917 when left-hander George Mogridge turned the trick against the Red Sox at Fenway Park. Mogridge issued three walks, and there were three Yankees errors. The Yankees snapped a 1–1 tie with a run in the ninth, and Mogridge set the Red Sox down in order to preserve the win and the no-hitter.

Six years later, Sad Sam Jones threw the second Yankees no-hitter. It was September 4, 1923, at Philadelphia. The 31-year-old stopped the Athletics 2–0. Jones walked one and did not strike out a batter during his moment in the sun.

Fifteen years went by before the next one occurred on August 27, 1938. It was the second game of a doubleheader against Cleveland, and right-hander Monte Pearson no-hit the Indians to the tune of 13–0. The Tribe would be victimized again by a Yankees pitcher a mere 13 years later.

But what made this one unique was that it was the first of two no-hit games tossed by this Yankees hurler in 1951. On July 12 Allie Reynolds threw a no-hitter to beat the Indians 1–0 at Municipal Stadium. What made the game even more remarkable was that

Yankees catcher Yogi Berra leaps into Don Larsen's arms after Larsen completed his perfect game in Game 5 of the 1956 World Series.

Reynolds beat Hall of Fame pitcher Bob Feller on Gene Woodling's solo home run in the seventh. The Chief walked three and set down the final 17 men in order for the first no-hit game that he threw in 1951.

The second historic outing came more than two months later. On September 28, in the first game of a doubleheader at Yankee Stadium, Reynolds threw his second no-hitter of the season as he beat Boston 8–0. The fire-balling righty became only the second major league pitcher to throw a pair of no-hitters in the same season—but it was not without its drama.

With two out in the ninth, Reynolds faced the great Ted Williams as his final challenge. With the count 0–1, Williams hit a foul pop fly behind the plate. Yankees catcher Yogi Berra settled under it and dropped it for an error to keep the at-bat alive.

Reynolds got Berra off the hook by getting Williams to do the same thing on the next pitch. This time Berra hung on, and Reynolds took a front page in the record books.

July 4, 1983

After Reynolds scored his second no-hit game of 1951, there wasn't another Yankees no-hit game for nearly 32 years.

Don Larsen's gem came in the World Series, but there was a void during the regular season. That shortage ended on July 4, 1983, at a very hot Yankee Stadium. David Allan Righetti was envisioned as the next great Yankees left-hander.

The 6'4" southpaw won the American League Rookie of the Year award in 1981 following an 8–4 record in the strike-shortened season with a sparkling 2.05 ERA. By 1983 the Yankees and many baseball fans expected Righetti to have a break-out season. When he

IF ONLY . . . Mike Mussina was able to get that 27th out on September 2, 2001, then he would have become the third Yankees pitcher in four years to have tossed a perfect game. Mussina set down the first 26 Red Sox hitters at Fenway that night before pinch-hitter Carl Everett broke up the bid with a single to left-center field.

warmed up to face the Red Sox in the holiday matinee, Rags was 9–3, but he had some added motivation.

Righetti had been left off the All-Star team after Ron Guidry bowed out due to injury. Rags seemed to be the likely replacement, but the American League determined that because he would be pitching on the final day before the break, Righetti would not be ready to pitch in the All-Star Game, so he was left off the team. The Red Sox would be the ones who felt Righetti's wrath.

You could tell from the very first inning that this was going to be a special day. Righetti came out on fire by striking out the side around a two-out walk to Jim Rice. Through three innings of work, Righetti allowed only one base runner, and he struck out seven of the 10 men he faced. Three more up and three more down in the fourth as Rags made it 10 straight hitters set down.

Meanwhile the Yankees were not faring much better against Boston starter John Tudor, who had given New York only two hits. The Yankees finally broke through in the fifth on an RBI single from Andre Robertson for a 1–0 lead.

Righetti was still rolling. The California-born left-hander walked Reid Nichols in the fifth but picked him off at first and then set the side down in order in the sixth.

Don Baylor's home run into the lower left-field stands in the Yankees half of the sixth made it a 2–0 lead. A one-out walk to Jim Rice in the seventh was quickly erased by a double play, and Righetti was six outs away.

Rags easily sailed through the eighth, and after the Yankees added two more runs to make it a 4–0 advantage, all that was left was to see if Righetti could do it. The crowd of more than 41,000 was standing, hoping to witness history.

Jeff Newman led off with a walk, but Glenn Hoffman forced Newman at second for the first out. Jerry Remy grounded out with Hoffman taking second, and it was left up to Wade Boggs, the Sox's most dangerous hitter. The great, left-handed hitter Boggs was the only thing that stood between Righetti and the record books.

The count was 2–2 when Rags looked at his catcher, Butch Wynegar, for the sign. Wynegar said, "I got down in my crouch and was ready to flash the fastball sign. Don't ask me why, but it suddenly came into my mind to call a slider."

"I wasn't looking for anything in particular," said Boggs. "Dave throws two types of sliders. I was just looking to keep the game going."

Rags was ready to go as the crowd roared its support. He delivered the slider. Boggs took a half swing, and he was gone. Home-plate umpire Steve Palermo signaled strike three, and Righetti had completed the pitcher's dream.

September 4, 1993

Left-hander Jim Abbott overcame much adversity to forge his major league career. He was a remarkable athlete. It wasn't remarkable that he was able to become a star collegiate player at Michigan and an Olympic Gold Medal winner in 1988. But it was remarkable that he did all of that without the benefit of a right hand. Abbott was born into adversity and overcame his handicap to live out his dream of pitching in the bigs.

Abbott mastered a method of fielding balls that served him well and laid to rest any fears that he could not make major league fielding plays. He delivered the pitch with the glove on his right forearm, then he transferred the glove to his left hand and made a play if need be, and then he reversed the process so that he could throw to first. On pickoff plays to first, he simply had the ball in his left hand the entire time, so all he had to do was toss it over to try and keep a runner close.

Abbott was being counted on for big things (after being acquired from the California Angels), but he struggled to a 9–11 mark entering the September game against Cleveland.

The Yankees were in a very tight race for the division title as they trailed first-place Toronto by only two games, so this was a big game for Abbott and the Bombers. It did not start well for the lefty as he walked Cleveland's leadoff hitter, Kenny Lofton. The southpaw fell behind the next hitter, Felix Fermin, but he turned a double play and a fly-out to work himself out of trouble.

A nasty slider was Abbott's signature pitch, and he couldn't have been throwing it any better in this one. Abbott kept his infield busy, and the Yankees offense took the cue, scoring three times in the third and once in the fifth on a solo home run from Yankees short-stop Randy Velarde, who would figure in the final out.

The left-hander got through the sixth, and the crowd began to sense something special was going on. "When it gets to the seventh, you start to count the outs," said Yankees right fielder Paul O'Neill. "Nine, eight, you begin to think this could really happen."

The seventh would be pivotal for Abbott.

With one out, Indians slugger Albert Belle hit a grounder toward the hole between short and third. Velarde would have had a difficult time throwing out Belle from the hole, but third baseman Wade Boggs cut in front of the shortstop with a diving stop to his left. The Hall of Famer then got up on his knees and threw out Belle to a thunderous standing ovation from the crowd.

Abbott had dodged a bullet on the way to history. After Boggs's saving play, a more routine ground ball to third ended the seventh. Six more to go.

In the eighth, Manny Ramirez struck out, and Abbott had reached a place where he had been before. Earlier in the season, Abbott was five outs away from a no-hitter against the Chicago White Sox at Yankee Stadium, but Bo Jackson ended the bid with a single. This time, Abbott got Candy Maldonado to bounce out to short for the second out. After a walk to Jim Thome, the southpaw put himself in position to go for it in the ninth after retiring pinch-hitter Sandy Alomar Jr. on a grounder to third.

The stage was set and the ninth inning provided a wide range of emotional swings.

"Everybody was afraid to jinx the thing," said Yankees manager Buck Showalter. "I had to go to the bathroom for four innings, but I was afraid to."

Yankees fans not only had the unique honor of rooting for such a grand achievement, but they were also rooting for the inspiration that Abbott was providing them.

Lofton led off the ninth and tried to lay down a bunt, but it went foul and so did the Yankees fans' moods as they heartily booed the Indians center fielder for a lack of baseball etiquette.

To the delight of the fans, Lofton bounced weakly to second for the first out.

TOP 10

All-Time Saves

1.	Mariano Rivera	413
2.	Dave Righetti	224
3.	Goose Gossage	151
4.	Sparky Lyle	141
5.	Johnny Murphy	104
6.	Steve Farr	78
7.	Joe Page	76
8.	John Wetteland	74
9.	Lindy McDaniel	58
10.	Luis Arroyo	43 †
	Ryne Duren	43 †

Fermin flied out to Bernie Williams in deep left-center field, so Cleveland was down to its final out with Carlos Baerga, the Indians second baseman. Baerga, a switch-hitter, batted right-handed in his first two unsuccessful at-bats against Abbott, but in his third time up, he hit left-handed against the southpaw pitcher so that he could get a better look at Abbott's devastating slider.

The look wasn't good enough as Baerga hit a grounder to short where Velarde fielded it cleanly and threw over to Don Mattingly for the final out.

Abbott faced first base, and after Mattingly caught the ball, the 6'3" lefty threw his arms up to his sides and awaited the wave of teammates that would engulf him.

When the mass of players and coaches subsided, Abbott took a satisfying walk toward the dugout arm in arm with Matt Nokes, his catcher, and the crowd cheered throughout.

After the game, Abbott said, "Every no-hitter takes a bit of luck." On this day, the lucky ones were those who watched it.

May 14, 1996

Dwight "Doc" Gooden once owned New York when he came up as a pitching phenom for the New York Mets in 1984. Gooden was on his way to a Hall of Fame career, but drugs and alcohol blocked the road to Cooperstown and the righty hurler was looking to make a comeback in 1996 after missing the entire 1995 season. Gooden made the Yankees out of spring training but was struggling to the tune of a 1–3 record and a 5.67 ERA.

The former National League Cy Young Award winner was practically out the door until David Cone was diagnosed with an aneurysm that would keep him out until September. Determined to turn Gooden around, pitching coach Mel Stottlemyre, who tutored Doc during his tenure with the Mets, decided to tinker with the 31-year-old's mechanics.

"We abbreviated his delivery so he gets to his release point earlier," said Manager Joe Torre. Gooden used this no-windup approach when he faced the Seattle Mariners at Yankee Stadium on May 14, 1996.

In the first, an omen of sorts occurred with the second batter of the game. Alex Rodriguez lined a shot toward center field where Gerald Williams went back on the dead run and made a great catch to snare the liner. No one knew it at the time, but that grab would be pivotal.

Gooden's command was so-so as he walked six, but he was able to work out of trouble against some pretty good Mariners hitters. There was a close call in the sixth when left fielder Darren Bragg hit one off of first baseman Tino Martinez's chest, but veteran official scorer Bill Shannon ruled that the play should be scored an error, and the crowd roared its approval.

The game was scoreless until the Yankees plated two runs in their half of the sixth on a sacrifice fly by Martinez and an RBI single from Jim Leyritz.

Three up, three down in the next two frames with Gooden getting Bragg on strikes to end the eighth. Now it was the ninth, and the crowd was on its feet to see if the former phenom could do it.

Rodriguez walked to open the inning, but Martinez took Ken Griffey's grounder and dove to the bag to record the out as A-Rod took second.

Noted Yankee killer Edgar Martinez walked. After a wild pitch put runners at second and third, Gooden struck out Jay Buhner with some "high heat" for the second out of the inning.

Some tinkering with his mechanics and delivery resulted in a no-hitter for Dwight Gooden (being carried) on May 14, 1996.

The next batter was left-hand hitting Paul Sorrento, who batted with the no-hitter and the game itself on the line.

This fairy tale had its happy ending when Sorrento popped out to shortstop Derek Jeter.

Gooden had pitched the ninth no-hitter in Yankees history and was triumphantly carried off the field by his admiring teammates in his moment of glory.

May 17, 1998

Left-hander David Wells always had the stuff to be a great pitcher, but he seemed to frustrate all the teams he played on. But for one game Wells put it all together, and that game became a signature moment in one of the greatest Yankees seasons of all time.

Wells's forte was control, and he could not have had better control as he took the mound against the Minnesota Twins that Sunday afternoon.

One, two, three became a familiar "dance step" for the Twins against the portly lefty. The only threat of a hit from the first nine hitters was a long fly ball down the left-field line off the bat of Twins catcher Javier Valentin that drifted foul.

Wells was getting a generous strike zone from home-plate umpire Tim McClelland and was taking full advantage of it as he struck out the first two batters in the sixth and then retired Pat Meares on a fly to center.

Minnesota leadoff man Matt Lawton flied to center to open the seventh. Brent Gates bounced out to first, and the burly southpaw faced his first crisis of the game. Wells fell behind the Twins designated hitter, Paul Molitor, but he battled back from a 3–1 count to strike out the Hall of Famer—and the anticipation level went up about 10 notches.

The eighth saw leadoff batter Marty Cordova ground out to short.

During a no-hit bid, there is usually a key defensive play that is made to preserve the gem. The next hitter, Ron Coomer, provided that moment as he laced one toward the middle that threatened to ruin the game for Wells. However, second baseman Chuck Knoblauch got a good jump on the ball, knocked it down, and threw Coomer out at first.

The 24th straight hitter that was retired was Alex Ochoa who popped out.

The Yankees had a 4–0 lead, and Wells went for the gusto.

The first hitter, Jon Shave, flied out to right, followed by a strikeout of Valentin—Wells's 11th of the game.

Pat Meares was all that stood between Wells and baseball history. On a 0–1 pitch, the Twins shortstop lifted a fly ball toward the right-field line. Right fielder Paul O'Neill, who had played in a perfect game with Cincinnati, corralled the 27th out as the crowd erupted.

Yankees broadcaster Jim Kaat called the final out on television. Kaat, a fellow left-hander who won 283 games in his major league career but never pitched a no-hitter, called Wells's perfect game the highlight of his broadcasting career.

Wells threw his arms out to his sides and awaited the reception.

"This is great Jorge, this is great," Wells said over and over to his battery mate, Jorge Posada. Darryl Strawberry and Bernie Williams, who was three for three in the game, carried the big southpaw off the field on their shoulders.

It was the 15th perfect game in baseball history and the second at Yankee Stadium, but it was the first ever in the regular season. It would not be the last.

July 18, 1999

Yogi Berra took the toss from Don Larsen. No, it wasn't a trip back in time to 1956. It was a re-enactment of the famous last pitch of Larsen's perfect game. As Yankees starting pitcher David Cone and catcher Joe Girardi admiringly looked on, Larsen's ceremonial "first pitch" to Berra was the highlight of Yogi Berra Day at Yankee Stadium, or was it? Cone and Girardi could not possibly have known that the final pitch of the game that the Yankees right-hander would throw to the veteran catcher would be one for the ages.

Unlike Berra in 1956, Girardi would not catch Cone's last pitch. That's because it would be a batted ball to end the game, but the result and the box score for the visiting team would read the same: 27 up, 27 down.

The interleague game against the Montreal Expos began with temperatures in the upper 90s, but Cone got off to a good start with a little help from his right-fielder Paul O'Neill.

After the former Cy Young Award winner got Expos designated hitter Wilton Guerrero for his first strikeout and the first out of the game, Montreal's Terry Jones lined a ball toward the gap in right-center field. O'Neill got an outstanding jump on it and dove to his glove side, rolling over as he made the catch.

A good baseball broadcaster would say "put a star on that one" in the hopes that maybe, just maybe, that catch saved an attempt at a no-hitter.

Rondell White flied out to Ricky Ledee in deep left field to end the first.

After Cone retired his next troika of hitters in the second, the Yankees put five runs on the board powered by a pair of monstrous two-run homers from Ricky Ledee and Derek Jeter.

In the top of the third, the skies opened up to the tune of a rain delay. Cone's stuff was really darting before the stoppage, but would he be working the same when he returned to the mound 33 minutes later?

TRIVIA

Which former Yankee wore the pinstripes for two perfect games and two no-hitters?

Answers to the trivia questions are on pages 186–187.

No problem as he finished the third by striking out the side. Cone then proceeded to set down the next 12 hitters to make it 21 in a row, capped off by a whiff from White for his eighth K.

Cone was masterful through seven, and he took that mastery into the eighth.

The leadoff hitter was Vladimir Guerrero, who fouled out to Girardi. The very tough Jose Vidro was next. With one out in the top of the eighth inning of David Wells's perfect game, Yankees second baseman Chuck Knoblauch made the key defensive play of the game when he moved to his right, stabbed a hot smash, and threw to first to preserve the gem.

It was one out in the top of the eighth in Cone's perfect game, and Vidro hit an eerily similar ball to the same position, second base, where Knoblauch made a terrific backhanded play to get to the ball and throw out Vidro at first.

After a play like that, maybe this *was* Cone's day.

"I went 2–0 on him," said Cone, who, up to that point, had not thrown two balls on any batter (nor would he the rest of the way). "He hit it hard up the middle, and I thought, *Here it goes.*"

Brad Fullmer struck out to end the eighth, and the pursuit of history was on.

With Larsen and Berra looking on, Cone went for the gusto. The Yankees added a run in the bottom of the eighth, and Cone began his final cadence of three. Chris Widger was Cone's 10th strikeout victim after a three-pitch effort. Pinch-hitter Ryan McGuire batted for Shane Andrews, and the left-hand hitter lifted a fly ball into short left field.

The famous "sunfield" at the Stadium was causing a bit of a problem for Ledee. Cone said, "I was worried he might have lost it," but Ledee had enough to corral the ball using two hands to make sure he caught it.

Twenty-six in a row. One out away from another great Yankees moment.

The batter was Orlando Cabrera, the Montreal shortstop. Cabrera was quoted afterward as saying, "If he throws a perfect game, I'm going to be the last out."

The 24-year-old native of Colombia swung and missed the first pitch. The second pitch was ball one to even the count. Then came the moment that only Larsen, Wells, and now Cone would experience as Yankees.

Cabrera lifted the next pitch into the air, in foul territory on the third-base side. "I was glad to see a pop-up and not some kind of weird ground ball," said third baseman Scott Brosius. Brosius caught the final out as Cone dropped to his knees only to be surrounded first by his catcher Girardi and then the rest of the team.

Close Calls

There have been a couple of close calls as well.

The most famous one came in Game 4 of the 1947 World Series. Yankees right-hander Floyd Bevens was leading 2–1 and was one out away from what would have been the first no-hitter in Series history when Dodgers pinch-hitter Cookie Lavagetto doubled in two to give Brooklyn a 3–2 victory.

In September of 2001 Mike Mussina set down the first 26 Red Sox hitters at Fenway Park and was one strike away from a perfect game when Boston pinch-hitter Carl Everett singled to break up the bid.

Subway Series: Yankees versus Mets

Throughout their history, the Yankees' chief rival has always been the Boston Red Sox.

But within the New York City limits, it is the Yankees and their National League cousins, the New York Mets, who rival for best-in-town accolades.

In today's baseball, with interleague play, the teams get to play each other every year. They also met in the 2000 World Series, an occurrence that, in the past, seemed as common as the weather changes throughout a New York City calendar year.

The "Subway Series" began in the 1920s when the Yankees played the New York Giants in three straight World Series matchups. The teams resumed their rivalry in the 1936 and 1937 Series, both won by the Yankees (who would defeat the Giants again in 1951). But in 1941 a new team took the Subway Series to new heights. The Brooklyn Dodgers won their first pennant since 1920, and they played the Yankees in the 1941 World Series.

It was the first of seven postseason meetings between the proud franchises. The Yankees went on to beat the Dodgers in 1941 and proceeded to do it again in 1947, 1949, 1952, and 1953 before finally succumbing to the "bums" in a seven-game thriller in 1955. Brooklyn finally had their victory over the Yankees, but the glory would be relatively short-lived. The Yankees avenged that loss in 1956, and after the following season, the Dodgers bolted New York for Los Angeles.

It marked the end of an era in New York baseball, as the New York Giants joined the Dodgers on the West Coast with a move to San Francisco.

In October 1960 the National League awarded expansion franchises to the cities of Houston and New York. The new Gotham entry in the National League would be known as the Metropolitans (Mets), and immediately the Mets tugged at the hearts of those National League fans who brooded over losing the Dodgers and Giants. It also created the new Subway Series, one that led to the resumption of an exhibition series between the intercity rivals called the Mayor's Trophy Game.

The Mayor's Trophy Game began in 1946 between the Yankees and the New York Giants with the proceeds from the game going to benefit the sandlot programs throughout New York City. The teams played an exhibition game once a year at an opportune time of the schedule that wouldn't hurt either club's chances with their own league pennant races. Brooklyn began participating in the series in 1951.

The games back then were taken pretty seriously, as is evidenced by a game between the Dodgers and Yankees at Yankee Stadium in July 1952. Most of the regulars, including Mickey Mantle, started and played the entire game, which lasted only eight full innings. The Yankees agreed to play until 11:00 PM because they had to catch a train to Cleveland. Mantle's error in the top of the eighth allowed the Dodgers to tie the game at three, but he smacked a two-run homer off Clyde King in the bottom half to win it.

Prior to the 1954 game, a home-run hitting contest was held between each team's best power hitters. Mantle hit two homers to give the Yankees a 7–6 win in the home-run derby. Jackie Robinson smacked three for Brooklyn, while Yogi Berra added two for the Bombers.

In early 1963, Mayor Robert F. Wagner announced that the first Mayor's Trophy Game between the Yankees and Mets would be played at Yankee Stadium on June 3. The game was rained out but rescheduled for the night of June 20. The unique thing about that date was that the Yankees had a regular-season game scheduled for that afternoon versus Washington at the stadium. It was almost a precursor

TRIVIA

Who played shortstop for the ninth inning of Game 7 of the 1960 World Series?

Answers to the trivia questions are on pages 186–187.

of what was to occur in 2000 when the Yankees played a day-night doubleheader with the Mets at two different ballparks. The Yankees won the game against Washington on a two-run, walk-off double from Bobby Richardson, but they lost to the Mets 6–2.

Shea Stadium hosted its first Mayor's Trophy Game in 1964, but not without a snag. The game was rained out and rescheduled for August. More than 55,000 fans were on hand to see the Yankees down the Mets, 6–4, behind home runs from Roger Maris, Tom Tresh, and Joe Pepitone, who blasted one off of the right-center-field scoreboard.

In the 1966 game at Shea, the Yanks had Hall of Fame southpaw Whitey Ford throw three innings. Ford had been nursing a sore elbow and returned to the active list in a relief role two days earlier. The left-hander went on to make his next start following the Trophy Game, but he would only start eight more times in his Yankees career before retiring in 1967. Ford actually came out of retirement to pitch in the 1968 Mayor's Trophy Game at Shea Stadium, and he tossed one scoreless inning.

Another rainout jeopardized the 1969 clash, which was originally scheduled for Shea Stadium just two days before Tom Seaver would throw his near-perfect game against the Chicago Cubs.

The Mets were already the National League's Eastern Division champions when they hosted and beat the Yankees on September 29. The game featured a "livelier" ball that was in use for the first five innings, and Yankees lefty Steve Hamilton's folly floater, a tantalizingly slow pitch, which was finally handled for a hard hit single by the Mets Tommie Agee.

In 1971 Hall of Famer Nolan Ryan started for the Mets in the Mayor's Trophy Game. Three months later, he would be dealt to the California Angels in one of the most infamous trades in baseball history.

The final Mayor's Trophy Game at the original stadium was played on August 24, 1972, as a young, 21-year-old right-hander named George "Doc" Medich went the distance in a 2–1 Yankees win. The victory evened the series at five games.

The games continued for the two-year period that both clubs played at Shea and resumed at the newly renovated Yankee Stadium in 1976.

Incidentally, in that 1976 game, the Yankees starting pitcher was Ron Guidry. Catfish Hunter made a pinch-hitting appearance and grounded out.

In what appeared to be the grand finale of the series, the 1979 game was a 1–1 tie that was washed out by rain after five innings.

The games were not played in 1980 and 1981 as both clubs cited scheduling problems, but they resumed in 1982 and 1983 before coming to a halt once again.

In January 1997 interleague play was approved on a two-year trial basis. For the first time in history, the New York Yankees would play the New York Mets in games that counted in the standings.

On June 16, a Monday night, history was made at Yankee Stadium as the Yankees and Mets played the first interleague game between the intercity rivals. It was the Mets who drew first blood. Dave Mlicki went the distance on a nine-hit shutout, and the Mets had a satisfying 6–0 victory.

The Yankees took Game 2, 6–3, and then they won the series with a thrilling 3–2 victory on a Tino Martinez walk-off single in the bottom of the tenth off of John Franco.

In 1998 the interleague play shifted to Shea for the first time. The opener saw the Mets holding a 3–2 lead in the seventh when Yankees right fielder Paul O'Neill slammed a three-run homer off of Mets reliever Mel Rojas, and the Bombers went on to an 8–4 win.

The Yankees won the second game, but the Mets avoided the sweep as Luis Lopez's sacrifice fly in the bottom of the ninth scored Carlos Baerga with the winning run in a 2–1 win.

The teams began an annual six-game schedule in 1999 with the first three at Yankee Stadium. The Yankees took two of three in the first series, but the rematch at Shea later that year proved to be eventful.

In Game 1, Mike Piazza hit a three-run homer off Roger Clemens to give the Mets a 5–2 victory and thus began a rivalry that spiced up the fans and the media for the next few years. The second game turned into an instant classic.

The Yankees hit six home runs and led the Mets 8–7 heading to the bottom of the ninth, and they had Mariano Rivera on the mound to close it. With two out and the bases loaded, pinch-hitter Matt

New York Mets catcher Todd Hundley slides safely around the tag of Yankees catcher Joe Girardi to score from third on a double steal during their first interleague game in 1997.

Franco batted for Benny Agbayani—and the rest is history. Franco singled off Rivera to score Henderson and Alfonzo with the winning runs in a 9–8 victory. The Yankees avoided being swept for the first time in the series as they scored a 6–3 win behind a solid outing from the much-maligned Hideki Irabu.

In 2000 the intercity rivalry reached new heights with a story line straight out of Hollywood capped off by the first real Subway Series since 1956. The teams split the first two games of a rain-shortened, interleague series, but the rainout would set up a historical show-down in July.

The teams were scheduled to meet again at Shea beginning on July 7. In order to make up the rained-out game at Yankee Stadium, a unique day-night doubleheader was set to be played on Saturday, July 8. The afternoon game would be the regularly scheduled game at Shea while the night game would be the make-up game to be played in the Bronx.

TOP 10

All-Time Runs Batted In

1.	Lou Gehrig	1,995
2.	Babe Ruth	1,971
3.	Joe DiMaggio	1,537
4.	Mickey Mantle	1,509
5.	Yogi Berra	1,430
6.	Bernie Williams	1,257
7.	Tony Lazzeri	1,154
8.	Bill Dickey	1,209
9.	Don Mattingly	1,099
10.	Bob Meusel	1,005

After winning the first game on Friday night, the Yankees turned to former Met "Doc" Gooden, who had been released earlier in the year by Tampa Bay. Gooden came back to haunt his old team as he pitched five innings in leading the Yankees to a 4–2 win over the Mets at Shea.

Following the game, the teams bused over to Yankee Stadium for the unique nightcap that was billed as "historic," but lived up to its billing for a totally different reason.

In the top of the second, Roger Clemens faced Mets catcher Mike Piazza and on a 0–1 pitch, the Rocket fired a fastball that caught Piazza solidly on the helmet, just below the bill.

The All-Star catcher fell to the ground on his back looking very much in a daze. Piazza wobbled as he left the field and headed for the clubhouse, but the Mets were incensed at the thought of Clemens using them for target practice.

Retaliation seemed inevitable.

In the bottom of the second, the Mets' Glendon Rusch plunked Yankees first baseman Tino Martinez in his backside, and home-plate umpire Ian Lamplugh issued a warning to both benches.

The Yankees won the game by the same exact score as the opener, 4–2, behind a three-run homer from Chuck Knoblauch.

These games were merely round one because the real fireworks would come in October as the two rivals were destined to meet for all the marbles.

The first Subway Series since 1956 would begin at Yankee Stadium on Saturday night, October 21. The city was buzzing with excitement and anticipation over this intercity rivalry reaching an all-time high. Game 1 was a classic as the Yankees rallied for a 4–3 win in 12 innings. The Mets had a 3–2 lead, but the Yankees tied the game in the bottom of the ninth and then won it on a single from former Met Jose Vizcaino.

Game 2 brought its own story line before a pitch was even thrown as Roger Clemens was scheduled to face the Mets for the first time since the beaning of Mike Piazza in July. Would the Mets retaliate under the spotlight of a World Series, and what about Piazza? It did not take long to find out.

After Clemens struck out the first two hitters, Piazza stepped into the batter's box. On a 1–2 pitch, Piazza swung and fouled the ball off, but he broke the bat into three separate pieces. One of the pieces floated out toward Clemens. He picked it up and flung it toward the first-base line where Piazza began to run. The broken piece did not hit Piazza, but no matter. The Mets catcher felt Clemens actually threw it at him.

Both benches emptied, but no fisticuffs broke out. And when order was restored, Piazza grounded out to second base on the ensuing pitch.

The Yankees took Game 2, 6–5, but the emotions of the two incidents would run high for years to come.

After the game, Clemens vehemently denied that he threw the bat shard at Piazza.

The Series shifted to Shea for Games 3, 4, and 5, and the Mets got back into it with a 4–2 victory in Game 3.

The Yankees won Game 4, 3–2, as Series MVP Derek Jeter set the tone with a leadoff home run off loser Bobby Jones.

In Game 5 the Yankees scored twice in the top of the ninth to take the Series with a 4–2 win.

What got the Mets even more upset was seeing the Yankees celebrate on their field. There was a

TRIVIA

Which Yankee made the last out of the Houston Astros' six-pitcher, no-hitter in 2003?

Answers to the trivia questions are on pages 186–187.

Manager Joe Torre holds the World Series trophy after the Yanks defeated the Mets in the 2000 Subway Series. Photo courtesy of Albert Coqueran.

plumbing problem with the visiting clubhouse at Shea, so the post-Series celebration was moved outside.

All these incidents contributed to keeping the emotions at a high level for the games to come between the two teams.

In 2001 the Yankees took four of six, but in 2002 the Mets and Yankees split the six games with the Flushing crew taking two of three at Yankee Stadium.

In 2003 the Yankees recorded the first sweep of the series as they won all six games. The slate included the second day-night, separate-site doubleheader.

The Mets finally got a measure of revenge in 2004. After losing two of three to the Yankees in the Bronx, the Mets swept the three-game series at Shea with Ty Wigginton's eighth-inning home run making the difference in the third game.

The gap between the clubs has narrowed, but the intensity between the teams and their fans never wanes.

Bonded by Pinstripe Glory

Throughout the Yankees' glorious history, there have been many memorable home runs, but only two players can lay claim to hitting a walk-off, pennant-winning home run while wearing the pinstripes. Chris Chambliss and Aaron Boone will be forever linked in Yankees history as the two who reached legendary status thanks to one swing of the bat.

The similarities of the two historic blows include both players leading off their fateful innings, both hitting the first pitch, both playing corner positions in the field, and both being acquired in trades with teams based in the state of Ohio.

Chambliss spent six seasons with the Yanks while Boone lasted less than a year. Early in the 1974 season, the Yankees engineered a seven-player trade with the Cleveland Indians. New York dealt pitchers Fritz Peterson, Fred Beene, Steve Kline, and Tom Buskey to Cleveland in exchange for pitchers Dick Tidrow and Cecil Upshaw plus a first baseman named Chris Chambliss.

During the 2003 season, the Yankees looked to fill a hole at third base. Scott Brosius announced his retirement after the 2002 campaign, so the Bronx Bombers were in need of someone to man the hot corner. On July 31, 2003, the Yankees acquired third baseman Aaron Boone from the Cincinnati Reds for two minor leaguers.

Let's examine both of the historic games by alternating between the two at similar junctures throughout.

October 14, 1976
A 31st American League championship was the prize awaiting the 1976 Yankees as they prepared to play the Kansas City Royals at

Yankee Stadium in a do-or-die, fifth-game showdown (from 1969 to 1984, the league championship series was a best of five).

Previous Yankees teams had played in these winner-takes-all contests in World Series play, but it was the first time the Bombers played for the American League pennant since baseball realigned into two divisions (East and West) for each league.

A best-of-five series that was hotly contested saw the Yankees win Games 1 and 3, while the Royals took Games 2 and 4.

Yankee Stadium would host its first deciding game of any kind since the 1957 World Series when the Bombers lost the seventh game to the Milwaukee Braves.

October 16, 2003

The theatrics featured in the rivalry of Yankees versus Red Sox reached a Tony Award–winning level with Game 7 of the 2003 American League championship series.

The teams battled mightily throughout the regular season, and thanks to the second realignment of major league baseball in 1995 (the first came in 1969 when the leagues split into two divisions), the Yankees won the American League's Eastern Division, while Boston qualified for the playoffs as the wild-card winner.

The teams met once before in postseason play as the Yanks took home their 36th pennant with a four-to-one victory in the 1999 American League championship series.

TRIVIA

Babe Ruth and Mickey Mantle hold the club records for most walks drawn in a season—Ruth for a left-handed batter and Mantle for switch-hitters. Which former Yankee holds the team record for walks drawn in one season by a right-handed hitter?

Answers to the trivia questions are on pages 186–187.

The Yankees won a one-game playoff in 1978 to decide the American League's Eastern Division title, but that was counted as a regular-season game, so this 2003 showdown would be the second time that the clubs would clash in the postseason.

The Yankees won the first two at Yankee Stadium while Boston rebounded to tie the series with a 9–6 win in Game 6.

The thought of Yankees versus Red Sox, Game 7, with the American

League pennant on the line, made baseball fans everywhere salivate with anticipation of what was to come. For the die-hard fans of the participants, it was nail-biting time.

Welcome to Yankee Stadium for Game 5 of the 1976 American League championship series.

Yankees manager Billy Martin looked to Ed Figueroa, a Puerto Rican–born right-hander who won 19 games in 1976 for the starting nod in Game 5. Kansas City skipper Whitey Herzog went with right-hander Dennis Leonard, who faced only three Yankees hitters.

The Royals drew first blood as John Mayberry hit a two-run homer off Figueroa in the first for a 2–0 lead. The Yankees answered with a first-inning rally of their own. Mickey Rivers tripled and scored on Roy White's single.

After a stolen base, Thurman Munson singled to left as the Yankees ended up with runners at second and third.

The Yankees added a second run in the first on a sacrifice fly from Chris Chambliss as noted Yankees killer—left-hander Paul Splittorff—relieved Leonard and limited the damage.

Kansas City took a 3–2 lead in the second on an RBI single from Buck Martinez, but the Bombers took the lead 4–3 in the third on a run-scoring single from Munson and an RBI ground-out by Chambliss.

A second run-scoring single by Munson and an error by Royals third baseman George Brett allowed the Yankees to grab a 6–3 lead in the sixth as they moved to within nine outs of the pennant.

Welcome to Yankee Stadium for Game 7 of the 2003 American League championship series.

The starting pitching matchup was front and center as two future Hall of Famers took the hill. Boston's ace Pedro Martinez against Yankees stopper Roger Clemens in what promised to be one for the ages, but it was Martinez who would become the focal point of the eventual outcome.

The first inning was scoreless, but in the top of the second the Red Sox took a 3–0 lead off Clemens. Noted Clemens nemesis Trot

Nixon clubbed a two-run homer into the right-center field bleachers, and Boston added a third run on an error by third baseman Enrique Wilson. The misplay was notable because it was Wilson who started over Boone because of his superior offensive numbers against Red Sox starter Martinez.

The fourth inning proved to be one of the turning points. Sox first baseman Kevin Millar homered to lead off the inning, so Boston had a 4–0 lead.

After Nixon walked, Bill Mueller singled to center to set up first and third with nobody out, and the Sox seemed primed to put this one away early. At this juncture, Yankees manager Joe Torre made the key strategic move of the game. He brought in starting pitcher Mike Mussina in relief to try and keep things under control. It was "all hands on deck" for a seventh game and Mussina was up to the task.

Big moment in the game. Top of the eighth, Yanks lead it 6–3. George Brett will bat, representing the tying run at the plate.

Figueroa pitched into the eighth when Royals right fielder Al Cowens singled to open the inning. Yankees skipper Billy Martin brought on southpaw Grant Jackson to face pinch-hitter Jim Wohlford who singled.

Two on, no one out, and the dangerous George Brett at the plate as the tying run.

The nightmarish situation became reality when Brett took a Jackson pitch and deposited it into the upper deck in right field for a game-tying three-run homer.

It was like a punch to the stomach for the stunned Yankees who found themselves in the eighth inning of a 6–6 tie in a do-or-die game for the American League pennant.

"The idea was to keep the ball in the ballpark," said Yankees catcher and 1976 American League Most Valuable Player Thurman Munson. "But just what we didn't want to happen, happened."

Jackson maintained his composure and went on to set down the Royals in the eighth, but the damage was done.

The Yankees went three and out in their half of the eighth. What was already a pulsating, dramatic show took the audience to the edges of their seats.

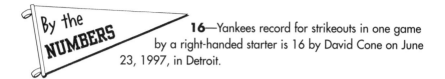

16—Yankees record for strikeouts in one game by a right-handed starter is 16 by David Cone on June 23, 1997, in Detroit.

Key moment of the game. Yanks trail the Red Sox 4–0 in the fourth, but the Bosox have first and third, no one out. Mike Mussina faces Jason Varitek.

Mussina began his stint by getting a huge strikeout of Sox catcher Jason Varitek.

Next up was the equally dangerous Johnny Damon, but in his previous two at-bats, he had hit the ball on the ground. The first time he was thrown out by shortstop Derek Jeter, but the second time Damon reached on an error by third baseman Enrique Wilson.

This time, Mussina was able to get Damon to slap into an inning-ending double play. Jeter scooped up a grounder that was headed toward center field, stepped on second, and fired to first to complete a huge "twin killing."

Meanwhile, the Yankees were not having much success with their longtime nemesis, Martinez. Pedro was setting the Bombers down with relative ease through the first four innings, but in the bottom of the fifth, Yankees designated hitter Jason Giambi led off with a home run to narrow the gap to 4–1.

Mussina kept the Red Sox at bay through the sixth, but the Yankees were still looking at a 4–1 deficit as they batted in the seventh.

Giambi's second home run of the game off Martinez gave the Yankees some life as the scoreboard now showed Boston 4, Yankees 2.

Yankees reliever Jeff Nelson retired Sox slugger Manny Ramirez on a ground out to third to start the top of the eighth.

Yankee killer David Ortiz was the next batter, so Torre decided to bring in left-hander David Wells. The strategy backfired when Ortiz took Wells deep into the right-field stands for a solo home run and a 5–2 advantage. For most teams, that would've broken their backs, but this was the Yankees versus the Red Sox, so unpredictability was the order of the day.

All-Time Team

One is the Loneliest Number: All-Time Yankees Team for Players Who Spent One Year or Less with the Yankees

Position	Name	Year with Yankees	Stats
C	Branch Rickey	1907	(.182, 0, 15)

Of course, Rickey will always be known for signing Jackie Robinson and breaking baseball's color barrier, but he was a back-up catcher for the New York Highlanders. On June 28, Rickey, who also played the outfield and first base, was victimized for a record-setting 13 stolen bases by the last place Washington Nationals.

1B	Johnny Sturm	1941	(.239, 3, 36)

Sturm was the leadoff hitter during Joe DiMaggio's 56-game hitting streak, yet he scored only 58 runs. He was drafted into the army in 1942 (World War II) and played only one season in the major leagues.

2B	Hack Simmons	1912	(.239, 0, 41)

George Washington "Hack" Simmons makes the team because throughout the history of the Yankees, they had very few second-sackers who played in only one season.

SS	Tony Fernandez	1995	(.245, 5, 45)

Fernandez was Derek Jeter's predecessor in 1995 and became the 14th Yankee to hit for the cycle.

3B	Aaron Boone	2003	(.254, 6, 31)

Boone hit one of the most significant home runs in team history when he led off the bottom of the eleventh inning of Game 7 against the Red Sox in the 2003 ALCS to give the Yankees their 39th American League pennant with a 6–5 win.

LF	Billy Sample	1985	(.288, 1, 15)

Sample played in 59 games for the 1985 Yanks, who made a surprise run at the AL East but lost out to Toronto on the final weekend of the season.

CF   George Halas   1919   (.091, 0, 0)

Yes, that George Halas. The famous NFL coach played 12 games (six in the outfield) for the Yankees. Halas, who was a switch-hitter, was 2 for 22 (.091) in his short stint as a big leaguer.

RF   Rocky Colavito   1968   (.220, 5, 13)

Colavito was signed as a free agent after being released by the Dodgers. The strong-armed outfielder once pitched for the Yankees and got the win in a game against his old Tigers team. Colavito played his final game in a Yankees uniform on September 28, 1968, which incidentally was also the final major league game for one Mickey Charles Mantle.

DH   Bobby Bonds   1975   (.270, 32, 85)

Bonds became part of two historic Yankees trades. First, in October 1974, center fielder Bobby Murcer was dealt to San Francisco for Bonds. After a year of unfulfilled expectations in New York, Barry's father was traded to the California Angels for center fielder Mickey Rivers and Ed Figueroa, both of whom went on to win World Series titles with the Yankees.

SP   Gaylord Perry   1980   (4–4, 4.44)

Perry went on to pitch 10 games for the 1980 Yankees after being acquired from Texas in August for right-hander Ken Clay.

RP   Jack McDowell   1995   (15–10, 3.93)

The reason a predominant starting pitcher gets the nod in relief is because he was the losing pitcher (in relief of Mariano Rivera) of the epic Game 5 American League division playoff loss in Seattle. McDowell gave up the game-winning hit to Edgar Martinez, which scored Ken Griffey Jr. with the winning run.

Manager   Dick Howser   1980   (103–59, first in AL East)

Howser was the only one-year Yankees manager to finish in first place. Howser was let go after being swept by the Kansas City Royals in the 1980 American League championship series.

Player's season stats are listed: AVG, HR, RBI. For the pitchers: Won-Lost record, ERA

TRIVIA

Former Yankees second baseman Alfonso Soriano made his big-league debut in 1999 and wore No. 66 to start the season. For how many games did Soriano wear No. 66?

Answers to the trivia questions are on pages 186–187.

The Bosox were five outs away from the American League pennant after Yankees first baseman Nick Johnson popped out to shortstop. If there was going to be any sort of miracle comeback, it had to start now.

Derek Jeter got things going with a double off the right-field wall. (Red Sox right fielder Trot Nixon actually misjudged the ball.) Yankees center fielder Bernie Williams then stroked a run-scoring single to center and it was 5–3.

At that point, it appeared that Martinez was beginning to tire, but Boston skipper Grady Little stayed with his ace, a decision that would come back to haunt him.

Little had left-hander Alan Embree warming in the bullpen, but he elected to let Martinez face Yankees left fielder Hideki Matsui. Matsui lined a double into the right-field corner to put runners at second and third with one out.

Martinez saw his final batter in Yankees catcher Jorge Posada, who promptly tied the game with a bloop double to center field.

Yankee Stadium erupted in a frenzy like never before. You could feel the ol' ballpark shake with joy as the fans celebrated this comeback. The game was tied and the best was yet to come.

A 6–6 tie and the Yankees will come to bat in the bottom of the ninth. Chris Chambliss will lead off.

Dick Tidrow replaced Grant Jackson to start the ninth, and after retiring the first two hitters fairly easily, Kansas City's Buck Martinez singled and Al Cowens walked, but Jim Wohlford forced Cowens at second to snuff out the potential rally.

There was a slight delay before Chambliss took his position in the batter's box, as the field was being cleared from debris from the fans. Royals pitcher Mark Littell took a few extra warm-ups.

"I never went up to the plate thinking about power too much because that would ruin my swing," Chambliss said. "I was just thinking about hitting the ball hard."

It was 11:43 PM Eastern time when Royals reliever Mark Littell delivered the famous pitch.

Yanks and Red Sox tied 5–5. Aaron Boone leads off the bottom of the eleventh. Mariano Rivera started the ninth and got through the inning unscathed.

Red Sox reliever Mike Timlin retired the Yankees in order, so the game went to the tenth.

Rivera got the first two outs in the tenth. David Ortiz doubled to left, but the former World Series Most Valuable Player retired Kevin Millar on a pop out to short.

The Sox went to knuckleballer Tim Wakefield to pitch the bottom of the tenth, and he set the Yanks down in order.

Rivera came out for an unprecedented third inning of work, but there was no tomorrow and the Yankees needed the absolute best out of their dominant closer.

Mo didn't disappoint as he recorded two strikeouts and a ground-out.

The Yankees came to bat in the bottom of the eleventh hoping to end it. Aaron Boone hit first in the eleventh. As Wakefield threw his warm-up pitches, the impending hero remembered something Yankees coach and former second baseman Willie Randolph had told him. "Willie told me before the series that I was his guy," said Boone nearly two years later. "When I got into the on-deck circle before my at-bat, Willie reminded me that I was his guy."

Wakefield was dazzling the Yankees with his dancing knuckler, and Boone was hoping to get something going.

"I didn't have much success against Wakefield," said the son of former major league catcher Bob Boone. "I'm walking up to the plate trying to get a pitch to hit."

Aaron Boone stepped into the batter's box.

The first pitch to Chamblis... Littell delivered a high fastball, and Chambliss got good wood on it. The ball sailed high in the air toward the right-center field wall.

Chris Chambliss (center) celebrates his historic ninth-inning home run that defeated the Kansas City Royals in the deciding game for the AL pennant in 1976.

Royals right fielder Hal McRae, sensing that this would be the game winner, went back to the wall and made a valiant attempt to try and make a play.

As the ball went over the wall, an 11-year gap without an appearance in the World Series had ended and a simultaneous and frantic procession of fans began pouring onto the field.

The brand-new Yankees hero started to make his way around the bases, but as he rounded first, a wave of people began to surround him.

"My first thought was that I hit a home run," said Chambliss. "Then I realized it was the ninth inning. The game was over, and we'd won the championship. Then I thought, *Oh no, the people are on the field.* I was in the middle of a mass of people, and when I fell to the ground it was scary." Chambliss slipped between second and third, but he regained his balance and tried to weave his way around toward home plate. But he couldn't get there before his helmet was ripped off his head and the big hulking first baseman knocked down one overzealous fan who was in the base line as he headed home. "I never felt like it was fun to celebrate that home run with the fans. They didn't belong on the field. I wanted to meet my teammates at home plate, and I couldn't," said Chambliss.

For the visiting Royals, it was like living a nightmare. "I didn't know what to do. I just headed toward our dugout," said losing pitcher Littell. "There were so many fans coming at me, but not one touched me. Somebody pulled my jersey and got me out of the dugout and into the runway."

The first pitch from Wakefield...

Not many people would have picked Aaron Boone to write the dramatic ending to a series of this magnitude. The storied rivals, the Yankees and the Red Sox. The seventh game of the American League championship series at the fabled Yankee Stadium. Bottom of the eleventh inning, tied at 5–5.

Boone did not have any thoughts of glory. "You're so consumed with the task at hand," he said. "I try and stay in the moment."

Wakefield's first pitch was his patented knuckler that shimmied toward the plate.

Before it could reach the mitt of Red Sox catcher Doug Mirabelli, Boone swung and sent it skyward toward the corner in deep left field.

Boston left fielder Manny Ramirez went back on it hoping for a play.

"When I hit it," said Boone, "I knew I got it. I was just hoping it would be fair."

It was past midnight on an October Friday when Boone's historic blast settled in the seats, prompting a celebration fit for New Year's

Aaron Boone's eleventh-inning home run defeated the Red Sox in Game 7 of the ALCS and propelled the Yankees to the World Series.

Eve. Unlike 27 years earlier, there were no fans on the field to "escort" Boone around the bases.

As he began his dream run around the bags, Boone could not totally recall what the trip was like. "It was a blur at first," said the Yankees third baseman, "but I tried to consciously tell myself to look around and savor the moment."

...and the fans have poured onto the field.
There was some doubt as to whether or not Chambliss did indeed touch home plate because no one could see his foot actually touch down on the dish, which was totally hidden by the mass of humanity that had settled on the field.

"I saw about 50,000 people touch home plate," said Thurman Munson. "He [Chambliss] could have been one of them. I'd like to see them take it back."

Chambliss's heroics were short-lived, however, as the Yankees were swept in the World Series by a terrific Cincinnati Reds team. But the memories of Chambliss's historic feat continue to be replayed many times over.

The stadium is rocking as Boone heads for home.
Boone rounded third and headed for home to be greeted by the entire Yankees team, which cleared a path for him to touch the dish with the winning run.

The second walk-off, pennant-winning home run was officially in the books, and the stadium cheers reached a higher decibel.

Like his predecessor's team in 1976, Boone's pennant-winning Yankees lost the World Series. This one in six games to the National League champion Florida Marlins.

It's hard to imagine a team being drained for a World Series, but you could make that argument, considering the emotional twists and turns that both the Yankees and Red Sox took during their epic encounters.

"Guys were emotionally drained," said Boone. "Game 1 we came out flat and could never totally recover."

Boone's heroics continue to be replayed over and over and over thanks to the magic of modern-day media. "I've seen it hundreds of times already," said Boone. "As I watch it, I understand that it will follow me for the rest of my life."

What couldn't be taken away was the name of Aaron Boone joining the ranks of pinstripe glory.

Frozen in Time: Moments That Fueled a Rivalry

The trade of Babe Ruth from Boston to the Yankees has been noted as the starting point of the greatest rivalry in sports.

The Yankees versus the Red Sox has made for great baseball drama and memorable moments over the years. However, to fully measure the impact of these annual confrontations is not to examine the numbers alone, but it is to reflect on those moments that these two clubs seemed destined to provide when they opposed each other.

Including the 2006 season, the numbers say that the two teams played 1,972 games with the Yankees holding a 1,076–882 edge along with 14 ties.

From the Curse of the Bambino to Bucky Dent's home run to Aaron Boone, the rivalry has not lacked for the ultimate in sports theater.

If you examine each team's record book, they have both provided the other with the "greatest comeback in franchise history."

The Yankees' greatest comeback spanned an entire 1978 season while in 2004 Boston's greatest rally spanned four incredible games with the Red Sox on the brink of elimination in each.

After the Ruth trade, the Bosox went into a funk in which they weren't a contender until the late 1930s. In 1938, 1939, 1941, and 1942, the Yankees and Red Sox finished one-two in the American League, but Boston never ended up better than nine games from the top in those years.

The Red Sox won the pennant in 1946 while the Yankees were 17 back in third place.

It wasn't until 1949 that the rivalry increased in its intensity. The Yankees and the Red Sox were locked in a classic pennant race that came down to the final day of the season. Boston led New York by one game with two to play, but those two were at Yankee Stadium to finish the season.

In the first game, Johnny Lindell's eighth-inning home run led the Yanks to a 5–4 victory that left both teams tied for first with one game remaining. The do-or-die showdown closed the season in dramatic fashion.

Behind 20-game winner Vic Raschi, the Yankees held a 1–0 lead but put up a four spot in the bottom of the eighth to blow the game open. The key hit was a bases-clearing double by second baseman Jerry Coleman.

The Yankees won the pennant, and the Red Sox took on a familiar role that they played in this rivalry many times over.

There were no dramatic pennant races between the teams for a long time after that, so the rivalry cooled a bit.

But even a year in which the Yankees finished in last place (1966) saw Boston right above them in ninth. The very next season, the Bosox made a stunning turnaround to win the American League pennant.

April 14, 1967. For the Yankees' home opener Boston was the opponent. A tall left-hander named Bill Rohr made his major league debut that day against a future Hall of Fame southpaw named Whitey Ford. The Yankees great pitched a solid eight innings, giving up three runs. But it was the neophyte who stole the show.

Rohr took a no-hitter into the ninth inning and had the hometown crowd on his side as he attempted to enter the record books.

Hall of Famer Carl Yastrzemski, who would be involved in many chapters of the storied rivalry, made a tremendous catch in left field to rob Tom Tresh of what would've been the first hit. Joe Pepitone flew out to right, and the young lefty was one out away. Elston Howard (who would be traded to Boston later that year) ran the count to 3–2 before placing a single in right field to spoil the bid. Rohr did not get the no-hitter, but the attempt seemed to inspire the Red Sox who went on to the World Series.

TOP 10

Most Runs Scored

1.	Babe Ruth	1,959
2.	Lou Gehrig	1,888
3.	Mickey Mantle	1,677
4.	Joe DiMaggio	1,390
5.	Bernie Williams	1,366
6.	Derek Jeter	1,277
7.	Earle Combs	1,186
8.	Yogi Berra	1,174
9.	Willie Randolph	1,027
10.	Don Mattingly	1,007

In the mid-1970s things heated up a little bit, particularly in 1975 when the Yankees and Red Sox competed for the AL East crown. Boston put the Yankees away in late July by sweeping a double-header at Shea Stadium buoyed by consecutive shutouts.

The fates of the two clubs were reversed in 1976 as Chris Chambliss hit a walk-off, three-run homer to beat Boston in a regular-season game played in late July. Chambliss went on to hit his dramatic pennant-winning home run later in the year.

In 1977 the teams battled each other in September, but the Yankees came out on top thanks to the heroics of Reggie Jackson who beat Boston in a pivotal regular-season game with a walk-off home run.

The story book finish of the 1978 American League East race provided goose bumps for Yankees fans and heartache for Boston. The Red Sox blew a 14½ game lead in July, and Bucky Dent joined New England's most-wanted list for the rest of time, or at least until 2004.

The Yankees returned to championship form in the late 1990s and so did the Bosox, who scratched and clawed their way to an ALCS matchup in 1999. It marked the first time that the two storied rivals would meet in a postseason series, and it certainly would not be the last.

IF ONLY . . . Tony Clark's ground-rule double had not bounced into the stands in Game 5 of the 2004 American League Championship Series. The Red Sox never would have made their incredible comeback. With two out in the top of the ninth of a 4–4 game at Fenway Park, Ruben Sierra walked and Clark scorched a double down the right-field line, but the ball went into the stands, leaving Sierra, who would have scored, at third. The next batter was Miguel Cairo who popped out to end the inning, and the Yankees went on to lose in 14 innings.

No one gave Boston a chance, but it took one of those breaks that the Yankees always seemed to get against the Bosox to help them take Game 1.

With the game tied at three in the top of the tenth, the Sox had a runner on first with no one out when John Valentin hit a grounder to third. Scott Brosius fielded it and fired to second to start a double play, but second baseman Chuck Knoblauch bobbled the ball as Jose Offerman arrived at second. Umpire Rick Reed ruled that Knoblauch was in the act of transferring the ball for a throw to first, thus the runner was called out at second. The Red Sox were furious because that helped snuff out a potential rally that ended when Brian Daubach grounded into an inning-ending double play.

Bernie Williams led off the bottom of the tenth with his second postseason walk-off home run. This one was a shot to dead center field off the Sox's Rod Beck, and it gave the Yanks a 4–3 win in Game 1. The Yankees took a 3–2 decision in Game 2 and headed to Fenway Park with a 2–0 lead in the series.

Game 3 provided a classic marquee matchup as Roger Clemens opposed the pitcher who would be named the AL Cy Young Award winner that year—Pedro Martinez. Martinez was brilliant, and Clemens was lousy as Boston routed the Yankees 13–1 to cut the series lead to 2–1.

The Bombers took Game 4 by blowing the game open with six in the ninth to coast to a 9–2 win. Ricky Ledee's grand slam was the big blow.

The Yanks coasted in Game 5 to a 6–1 victory behind seven solid innings from Orlando "El Duque" Hernandez. The win allowed the Yanks to clinch their 36th American League championship while they danced on Boston's graves by celebrating on their field.

The rivalry really took on a whole new intensity when the teams met for the second time in the 2003 American League championship series. There were story lines galore for the press to digest, not to mention some great baseball. The teams split the first two games at Yankee Stadium, and Game 3 was a rematch from four years prior. Roger Clemens against Pedro Martinez with a whole new set of circumstances surrounding the encounter.

There was a near bean brawl and a real bean brawl that culminated when Martinez threw Yankees coach Don Zimmer to the ground in front of the Boston dugout. In the fourth, Yankees outfielder Karim Garcia was hit by Martinez, who began "jawing" with the slim right-hander. In the home half, Manny Ramirez did not like the fact that Clemens came in high and hard, so he took a few steps toward the mound, which incited another bench-clearing mêlée. In the end, the Yankees and Clemens won the game 4–3 as Rocket outdueled Pedro.

Boston evened the series with a Game 4 win, but the Yanks took Game 5 behind the pitching of David Wells and Mariano Rivera.

TOP 10

Most Games Played As a Yankee

1.	Mickey Mantle	2,401
2.	Lou Gehrig	2,164
3.	Yogi Berra	2,116
4.	Babe Ruth	2,084
5.	Bernie Williams	2,076
6.	Roy White	1,881
7.	Bill Dickey	1,789
8.	Don Mattingly	1,785
9.	Joe DiMaggio	1,736
10.	Willie Randolph	1,694

The Red Sox wouldn't go quietly as they took Game 6 thanks to some embarrassing play by the Yankees, who had a 6–4 lead going to the seventh.

The stage was set for Game 7, and Aaron Boone walked off as the latest Yankees hero from the eventful and exciting meetings.

Two thousand and four marked the third meeting in five years between the two, and a whole new bizarre chapter of this historic showdown was written with Boston's ink and the Yankees' blood.

The Yanks jumped to a 3–0 series lead and appeared to be headed to their 40th World Series, but a funny thing happened on the way to the Fall Classic. The Red Sox staged the greatest comeback in postseason baseball history as they rallied from three games down to stun the Yankees and win the pennant with a Game 7 rout at Yankee Stadium.

Bernie Williams nearly signed with Boston after the 1998 season but went on to play a key role for the Yankees in their rivalry with the Sox. Photo courtesy of Albert Coqueran.

The Curse of the Bambino was no more. The Sox had seen to that by beating the Yankees in as a dramatic fashion as you can get and then finally winning their elusive World Series.

In 2005 the rivalry picked right up where it left off. The Yankees got off to a slow start and trailed the Red Sox for just about the entire season in the race for the American League East title. New York surged back and led the Red Sox by a game in September with a three-game series set for Fenway Park.

Boston won the opener, so the teams were tied with two to play. Yankees starting pitcher Randy Johnson was not at his best, but he was good enough to help the Yanks clinch the division (because of American League tiebreakers, the Yankees clinched even though they led by one game with one to play) for the eighth straight season.

The Final Out

Imagine that you are on the field for the ninth inning of the final game of the World Series, and you're three outs away from winning it. A chance to grab the final out of the World Series is at hand and what a feeling it must be when you make that catch and know that you're a champion.

The New York Yankees have experienced that feeling many times before. In fact, out of their 26 World Series championships, the Yankees have had that feeling exactly 24 times in their glorious history.

If you take away the 1927 and 1953 World Series victories, where the Yankees won on a walk-off wild pitch and single respectively, there have been 24 chances for players or pitchers to record the final out. The final-out numbers read like this: seven ground-outs, including a double play, nine fly-outs, three strikeouts, three pop-ups, and two lineouts, one of which provided one of the most famous endings in Series history in 1962.

The Yankees and San Francisco Giants waged quite a battle as the Series went the full seven games. New York held a 1–0 lead in Game 7 heading to the bottom of the ninth. Yankees right-hander Ralph Terry was pitching brilliantly into the ninth, but the Giants staged a rally. With two out, San Francisco had runners at second and third, and the dangerous Willie McCovey was at bat. With another dangerous hitter in Orlando Cepeda on deck, the Yanks elected to pitch to McCovey.

While Ralph Houk spoke with his pitcher, second baseman Bobby Richardson spoke to shortstop Tony Kubek. Kubek kiddingly said to his keystone partner, "I hope they don't hit it to you. You've already made an error in this Series."

By the
NUMBERS

11—Number of Yanks who have made final out of a series

1921: Frank "Home Run" Baker (3B) hits into a 4–3–5 double play; Giants Johnny Rawlings (2B) to George "High Pockets" Kelly (1B) to Frankie Frisch (3B), who tagged out Aaron Ward

1922: Aaron Ward (2B) flied out to Giants Ross Youngs (RF)

1926: Ruth ends the Series attempting to steal second but is thrown out, Cards Bob O'Farrell (C) to Rogers Hornsby (2B) (Note: the pitcher was Grover Cleveland Alexander, who was a 39-year-old reliever)

1942: George Selkirk (PH) grounds out to second; Cards Jimmy Brown (2B) to Johnny Hopp (1B)

1955: Elston Howard (LF) grounds out to Dodgers Pee Wee Reese (SS) to Gil Hodges (1B)

1957: Moose Skowron (1B) forces Jerry Coleman at third with two out and the bases loaded as Braves Eddie Matthews (3B) steps on the bag for the final out

1960*: Pirates Bill Mazeroski (2B) with the famous walk-off, series-winning home run against Ralph Terry

1963: Hector Lopez (RF) grounds out to Dodgers Maury Wills (SS) to Moose Skowron (1B)

1964: Bobby Richardson (2B) pops to Cardinals Dal Maxvill (2B)

1976: Roy White (LF) flied out to Reds George Foster (LF)

1981: Bob Watson (1B) flies out to Dodgers Ken Landreaux (CF)

2001*: D-Backs win on walk-off single from Luis Gonzalez (LF) against Mariano Rivera

2003: Jorge Posada (C) hits a weak bouncer back to the mound where Marlins Josh Beckett (P) fields it and tags Posada for the unassisted putout

*Yanks lost series in opponent's at-bat

Terry delivered the first pitch and McCovey got a good swing on it, but he drove it foul down the right side. Right before the next pitch was thrown, Richardson said second-base umpire Al Barlick asked if he could have his cap once the game ended. McCovey then smacked a vicious line drive right at Richardson. Richardson squeezed it, and the Yanks were champs for the 20th time.

TOP 10

Doubles

1.	Lou Gehrig	535
2.	Bernie Williams	449
3.	Don Mattingly	442
4.	Babe Ruth	424
5.	Joe DiMaggio	389
6.	Mickey Mantle	344
7.	Bill Dickey	343
8.	Bob Meusel	338
9.	Tony Lazzeri	327
10.	Yogi Berra	321

After the game, Richardson was relieved that he had caught the final out. Richardson said, "If McCovey's line drive had taken off, I might have been in trouble." By the way, he did toss his cap to the umpire.

A lineout also ended the 1939 World Series against the Cincinnati Reds. The Yankees scored three runs in the top of the tenth to take a 7–4 lead. With two on, and the tying run at the plate against Yankees reliever Johnny Murphy, the Reds Wally Berger lined one toward short, but Frank Crosetti hauled it in for the victory.

There have been numerous Hall of Famers associated with the final outs of Yankees World Series victories and defeats.

In 1926 Babe Ruth was thrown out trying to steal second to end that seven-game Series against St. Louis. But in 1928 Cardinals second baseman Frankie Frisch lifted a Series-ending fly ball to left that was caught by Ruth.

In 1947 it was a double play that turned out to be the Series clincher in Game 7. The Yankees led 5–2 in the bottom of the ninth, but the Dodgers had a runner on base. Yankees reliever Joe Page got Brooklyn catcher Bruce Edwards to bounce to Phil Rizzuto at short. Rizzuto flipped to Snuffy Stirnweiss at second with the relay to George McQuinn to complete the "twin killing" and end the Series.

Page was on the mound again in 1949 when he struck out the Dodgers' Gil Hodges to end Game 5 and the Series for the Yankees.

Johnny Murphy and Bob Kuzava, a crafty left-hander, both were Series-finishing pitchers twice in their Yankee careers. The only Yankees pitcher to be on the hill three times for Series-clinching wins is Mariano Rivera, who turned the trick in a three-year span from 1998 to 2000.

Rivera pitched in the 1996 clincher but did not finish. The closing duties that year were handled by hard-throwing righty John Wetteland, who got the Braves' Mark Lemke to foul out to third baseman Charlie Hayes, as the Yanks ended an 18-year drought without a title.

In 1998 the Yankees were like a juggernaut as they muscled their way to the Series against San Diego. A four-game sweep was in order. Rivera ended this one by getting Padres pinch-hitter Mark Sweeney

Mariano Rivera displays his World Series MVP award after recording the final out of the 1999 sweep of the Braves. Photo courtesy of Albert Coqueran.

26—Number of Yankees who have recorded the final play of a World Series win.

Who Recorded the Out, How It Was Done, and Who the Pitcher and Hitter Were

1923: Aaron Ward (2B) to Wally Pipp (1B); Sad Sam Jones (P); New York Giants Jack Bentley (PH)

1927*: Earle Combs scores on a wild pitch in ninth inning of Game 4

1928: Babe Ruth (fly-out to LF); Waite Hoyt (P); Cardinals Frankie Frisch (2B)

1932: Ben Chapman (fly-out to RF); Herb Pennock (P); Cubs Riggs Stephenson (LF)

1936: Lou Gehrig (1B) (unassisted putout at 1B); Johnny Murphy (P); Giants Harry Danning (C)

1937: Lou Gehrig (1B) to Lefty Gomez covering 1B; Gomez (P); Giants Jo Jo Moore (LF)

1938: Red Ruffing to Gehrig; Ruffing (P); Cubs Billy Herman (2B)

1939: Frank Crosetti (SS) caught a line drive in tenth inning; Johnny Murphy (P); Reds Wally Berger (CF)

1941: Joe DiMaggio (fly-out to CF); Tiny Bonham (P); Dodgers Jimmy Wasdell (PH)

1943: Joe Gordon to Nick Etten (ground-out 4–3); Spud Chandler (P); Cards Debs Garms (LF)

1947: Double play (Phil Rizzuto–Snuffy Stirnweiss–Geo McQuinn, 6–4–3); Joe Page (P); Dodgers Bruce Edwards (C) **seventh game

1949: Joe Page (P) strikes out Dodger Gil Hodges (1B); Yogi Berra (C) gets final putout

1950: Phils Stan Lopata (PH) struck out against Allie Reynolds (P); Yogi Berra (C) gets final putout

1951: Hank Bauer (lineout to RF); Bob Kuzava (P); Giants Sal Yvars (PH)

1952: Gene Woodling (fly-out to LF); Bob Kuzava (P); Dodgers Pee Wee Reese (SS) ** seventh game

1953*: Billy Martin wins Series with walk-off single, scoring Hank Bauer, in Game 6

1956: Johnny Kucks (P) strikes out Dodger Jackie Robinson (3B); Berra to Skowron (1B) on the putout

1958: Mickey Mantle (fly-out to CF); Bob Turley (P); Braves Red Schoendienst (2B) ** seventh game

1961: Hector Lopez (fly-out to LF); Bud Daley (P); Reds Vada Pinson (CF)

1962: Bobby Richardson (lineout to 2B); Ralph Terry (P); Giants Willie McCovey (LF) ** seventh game

1977: Mike Torrez fields final out on a bunt pop out to the mound; Torrez (P); Dodgers Lee Lacy (PH)

1978: Thurman Munson (C) catches foul pop out behind the plate; Rich Gossage (P); Dodgers Ron Cey (3B)

1996: Charlie Hayes (3B) catches foul pop-up to John Wetteland (3B); Braves Mark Lemke (2B)

1998: Tino Martinez (1B) from Scott Brosius (5–3 ground-out); Mariano Rivera (P); Padres Mark Sweeney (PH)

1999: Chad Curtis (fly-out to LF); Rivera (P); Braves Keith Lockhart (DH)

2000: Bernie Williams (fly-out to LCF); Rivera (P); Mets Mike Piazza (C)

* Yanks were at bat when Series ended.

to ground to Series Most Valuable Player Scott Brosius at third who threw to Tino Martinez at first for the final out.

In 1999 the Yankees completed a four-game sweep of the Braves with Rivera retiring Atlanta's Keith Lockhart on a fly-out to left fielder Chad Curtis.

Once again, Rivera was on the hill for the final out of the Subway Series in 2000 when he got Mike Piazza to hit a deep fly ball to the wall in left-center field. Bernie Willliams made the catch as the Yankees beat the Mets in five games to capture their 26th world title.

Of course, when you win so many pennants, there are long odds to winning every World Series that you play in. Thusly, the Yankees have found themselves on the short end of 13 fall classics.

So who made the final outs for the Yankees in those defeats? Out of the 13 Series losses, there were three instances where a Yankees batter did not hit into a final out.

One was when Ruth was thrown out stealing, and two were devastating walk-off defeats. The first was in 1960 when Pittsburgh

Pirates second baseman Bill Mazeroski hit his famous walk-off World Series–winning home run in the bottom of the ninth inning of the seventh game.

The second time occurred with Mariano Rivera on the mound in 2001 as Arizona rallied in the bottom of the ninth of the seventh game to pull off a stirring comeback victory and stun the Yankees, who were seeking their fourth-straight World Series crown. Those final-out numbers say six ground-outs (including a double play), three fly-outs, and one pop out. Interestingly, no Yankee ever struck out to end a World Series.

One former Yankee actually made the final out of a Yankees defeat and also caught the final putout for a Yankees defeat. Bill "Moose" Skowron was the Yankees first baseman in 1957 when he bounced into a game- and Series-ending force play at third base in the ninth inning of the seventh game at Yankee Stadium. Six years later, Skowron was playing first for the Los Angeles Dodgers when he caught the final putout on a throw from Maury Wills as the former Brooklyn Bums swept the Yankees in four games.

Ruth was thrown out trying to steal by Cardinals catcher Bob O'Farrell to end the 1926 Series. At the time, many thought that Ruth had lost his mind. The Yankees trailed 3–2 when Babe walked with two out. Bob Meusel was at bat but did not have a home run or run batted in for the entire Series, which is probably why Ruth took off. No matter, the Babe provided one of the most unusual Series endings in baseball history.

Third baseman Home Run Baker ended the 1921 Series by grounding into an unusual 4–3–5 double play. The next year second baseman Aaron Ward, who was tagged out at third on the final play of the 1921 Series, made the last out against the Giants by flying out to Ross Youngs in right field.

Let's Make a Deal: Best and Worst Trades in Yankees History

Baseball trades have been as much a part of the sport as home runs. For years, fans have debated the merits of a deal, with a keen eye on how it affects their favorite team. In Yankees history, a long litany of transactions has been consummated, both good and bad. Here's a breakdown of the best and worst trades in Yankees history (in no particular order).

The Best
January 3, 1920
Yanks acquire Babe Ruth from the Red Sox in exchange for $125,000 and a $350,000 loan against the mortgage of Fenway Park. The Bosox were vilified for this trade until they finally won another World Series title in 2004.

Trade Wins: Many observers consider this the most one-sided trade in baseball history. To define how much this deal impacted not only the Yankees but also baseball itself, you need only remember the monikers of Ruth: Big Fella and Babe.

December 11, 1959
Yanks acquire outfielder Roger Maris, infielder Joe DeMaestri, and first baseman Kent Hadley from the Kansas City Athletics in exchange for outfielders Norm Siebern and Hank Bauer, along with pitcher Don Larsen and first baseman Marv Throneberry. The 25-year-old Maris was the key to the trade. The Yankees figured that his sweet left-handed swing would be tailor-made for the short right-field porch at Yankee Stadium.

DeMaestri and Hadley never panned out. Siebern was a highly touted rookie prospect with the Yanks in 1956 but injuries ruined his career.

Larsen would forever be known as the man who threw the perfect game in the World Series while Bauer's career fizzled after being dealt from New York.

Throneberry went on to infamy as a member of the expansion New York Mets in 1962.

Trade Wins: The Yankees figured right as Maris went on to win two Most Valuable Player awards and set the baseball world on fire while breaking Ruth's record in 1961.

October 11, 1946

Yanks acquire right-handed pitcher Allie Reynolds from Cleveland in exchange for second baseman Joe Gordon. The 31-year-old Gordon had given the Yanks six solid seasons before a two-year stint in the service. When he returned, Gordon was not the same player. The Yankees had an abundance of middle infielders, including Phil Rizzuto, so they dealt from strength. The Indians, who had a surplus of starting pitching, deemed the Oklahoma-born Reynolds expendable.

Trade Wins: The 6', 190-pound right-hander, aka "Super Chief" because of his Native American heritage, went on to be one of the best Yankees pitchers of all time.

Gordon played four seasons for Cleveland and then was traded to Detroit in 1960 for Jimmy Dykes in a swap of managers.

December 11, 1975

Yanks acquire outfielder Mickey Rivers and right-handed pitcher Ed Figueroa from the California Angels in exchange for outfielder Bobby Bonds.

This deal became one of the two key trades (which were made on the same day) that helped the Yankees win the American League pennant in 1976. Rivers was a sparkplug at the top of the order for the Yankees while Figueroa went on to become the first Puerto Rican–born pitcher to win 20 games. Bonds had his best year as a big leaguer with the Angels in 1977, but after that he was never the same player.

By the NUMBERS

9—Number of Yankees who have won a batting title

Name	Year	Batting Average
Babe Ruth	1924	.378
Lou Gehrig	1934	.363
Joe DiMaggio	1939	.381
Joe DiMaggio	1940	.352
George Stirnweiss	1945	.309
Mickey Mantle	1956	.353
Don Mattingly	1984	.343
Paul O'Neill	1994	.359
Bernie Williams	1998	.339

Trade Wins: Bonds lasted one year with the Yanks after being acquired for Bobby Murcer. Rivers became one of the Yanks' best "table setters" while Figueroa became a staple of the rotation for several years.

December 11, 1975

Yanks acquire second baseman Willie Randolph, left-handed pitcher Ken Brett, and right-handed pitcher Dock Ellis in exchange for right-handed pitcher George "Doc" Medich.

The Yankees badly needed a second baseman to stabilize the infield, and Randolph became one of the Yanks' best. Ellis went 17–8 in 1976 but was traded to Oakland in April 1977. Brett (brother of Hall of Famer George Brett) appeared in only two games as a Yankee and was traded in April 1976 to the Chicago White Sox for designated hitter Carlos May.

Medich pitched one season for the Pirates, posting an 8–11 mark and was traded during spring training of 1977.

Trade Wins: Medich was never the same and while Ellis and Brett were not long-term solutions, Randolph's acquisition puts this deal in the top echelon of best Yankees trades.

April 26, 1974

Yanks acquire first baseman Chris Chambliss and pitchers Cecil Upshaw and Dick Tidrow from Cleveland in exchange for pitchers Fritz Peterson, Tom Buskey, Steve Kline, and Fred Beene.

Chambliss was another piece to the puzzle. He became a steadying influence and contributed some big hits to a pair of World Series championship teams. He was best known for his pennant-winning home run that beat the Royals in the 1976 ALCS. Tidrow was a valuable member of the pitching staff for six years including 1978 when he started 25 games in place of some injured starting pitchers that season. Upshaw was in pinstripes for one season.

The four hurlers sent to Cleveland all had something in common. They all fizzled after the trade.

Trade Wins: Most observers thought that the Yanks gave up too much, but Chambliss's left-hand swing and ability at first base proved to be a huge asset to the two-time World Series champion Yankees of the 1970s.

November 3, 1992
Yanks acquire outfielder Paul O'Neill from the Cincinnati Reds for outfielder Roberto Kelly. This is one of the most underrated deals in Yankees history.

The 1992 trade that landed Paul O'Neill (batting) from Cincinnati for outfielder Roberto Kelly was one of the most underrated deals in franchise history. Photo courtesy of Albert Coqueran.

O'Neill had a magnificent Yankees career as one of the key cogs that won four championships in five years.

Kelly was dealt to six more teams after Cincinnati before one more short stint in pinstripes, but he never lived up to his potential.

TRIVIA

Who holds the Yankees career record for most pinch-hit home runs?

Answers to the trivia questions are on pages 186–187.

Trade Wins: O'Neill had a "rap" of not being able to hit left-hand pitching, but he dispelled that notion while with the Yankees. His fire and energy in the dugout was one of the Yankees trademarks during their remarkable late 1990s run. This was considered the "bookmark" deal that catapulted the Yankees back to being one of baseball's elite teams.

Other "Best" Deals

July 28, 1995
Yanks acquire right-handed pitcher David Cone from the Toronto Blue Jays in exchange for pitchers Marty Janzen, Jason Jarvis, and Mike Gordon.

November 18, 1997
Yanks acquire third baseman Scott Brosius from the Oakland Athletics as the player to be named later in exchange for left-handed pitcher Kenny Rogers, who was traded on November 7.

March 22, 1972
Yankees acquire left-handed pitcher Sparky Lyle from Boston in exchange for first baseman Danny Cater and infielder Mario Guerrero.

November 17, 1954
Yanks acquire pitchers Don Larsen and Bob Turley, infielder Billy Hunter, and four minor leaguers in exchange for outfielder Gene Woodling, shortstop Willie Miranda, catchers Gus Triandos and Hal Smith, and pitchers Harry Byrd and Jim McDonald, plus four minor leaguers.

December 7, 1995

Yanks acquire first baseman Tino Martinez along with pitchers Jeff Nelson and Jim Mecir from the Seattle Mariners in exchange for third baseman Russ Davis and left-handed pitcher Sterling Hitchcock.

The Worst

December 9, 1982

Yankees trade outfielder Dave Collins, pitcher Mike Morgan, and first baseman Fred McGriff to Toronto for pitchers Dale Murray and Tom Dodd.

The left-hand slugger McGriff would've put up some terrific numbers playing at Yankee Stadium. Unfortunately, it wasn't to be as the Yankees penchant for giving up too quickly on young talent really came back to bite them this time.

Collins was brought to the Yankees to provide some speed, which he produced with a grand total of 13 steals. The remainder of his career was not much to brag about.

Morgan continued his career until 2002, playing for 10 more teams after being traded from New York.

Murray did not distinguish himself in pinstripes. Dodd never threw a pitch for the Yankees.

Trade Losses: This set the tone for a long string of bad moves made by the Yankees in the 1980s.

July 21, 1988

Yankees send outfielder Jay Buhner and pitcher Rich Balabon to Seattle for designated hitter Ken Phelps.

This deal is probably best known for providing steady fodder for a popular TV sitcom, *Seinfeld*.

The Yankees wanted Phelps to boost their left-hand power, but they failed to realize that their former number-one draft pick (11th overall in 1974 but he did not sign) was not a "dead pull" hitter. He failed to take advantage of Yankee Stadium's short right-field "porch," instead hitting a lot of long fly-outs.

Buhner played 13 full seasons with Seattle, where he constantly reminded the Yankees that they never should have traded him.

Trade Losses: The Gold Glove–winning Buhner had a rocket arm and was superbly suited for right field. The Yankees had "stolen" Buhner from Pittsburgh in a trade for Steve Kemp.

December 8, 1966

Yankees trade outfielder Roger Maris to the St. Louis Cardinals for third baseman Charley Smith.

The Yankees could not get anything of real value for Maris. That was the company line after the single-season home-run champ struggled through two injury-plagued seasons in 1965 and 1966.

Nine days previous, the Yankees traded third baseman Clete Boyer to Atlanta for outfielder Bill Robinson, so they took Smith from the Cards for Maris to fill the void.

Trade Losses: Maris's contract was what probably got him traded, but he made a major contribution to two pennant winners and a world championship in St. Louis during his two-year stint.

October 21, 1981

Yankees trade outfielder Willie McGee to St. Louis for pitcher Bob Sykes. The Yanks had egg on their faces after this deal.

Despite good numbers and a solid work ethic, the Yanks felt McGee would never grow out of the inconsistencies that he showed at every level in the minors. Sykes never threw a pitch for the Yankees.

Trade Losses: The embarrassment of this deal was felt for a long time. Less than a year after the trade was made, McGee hit two home runs in Game 3 of the 1982 World Series to help the Cards beat the Brewers.

The former Yankees prospect took home the National League's Most Valuable Player award in 1985 and was also a three-time Gold Glove winner in the outfield.

TRIVIA

Cliff Mapes wore Mantle's No. 7 before Mickey had it. Mapes wore another retired Yankees number after this player had finished his Yankees career (before the number was put out for good). Name this Yankees great.

Answers to the trivia questions are on pages 186–187.

TRIVIA

What number did Mickey Mantle wear when he broke in during the 1951 season?

a) 2
b) 9
c) 10
d) 6

Answers to the trivia questions are on pages 186–187.

November 26, 1962
Yankees trade first baseman Bill "Moose" Skowron to the Dodgers for right-handed pitcher Stan Williams.

This trade stunned most Yankees observers. Skowron had given the Bombers nine straight years of steady production and better-than-average fielding at first base, and he came off a year where he smacked 23 home runs and drove in 80.

Williams pitched to a 10–13 mark over two years in the Bronx and was sold to Cleveland in March 1965.

Trade Losses: Skowron got his payback in less than a year when he faced the Yankees as the first baseman for the Los Angeles Dodgers in the 1963 World Series. Moose contributed a home run in the Game 2 win at Yankee Stadium and recorded the final putout on a grounder to short as the Dodgers completed a four-game sweep.

Other Worst Deals

August 29, 1951
Yankees trade right-handed pitcher Lew Burdette to Boston Braves for right-handed pitcher Johnny Sain.

June 15, 1976
Yanks trade pitchers Rudy May, Scott McGregor, Tippy Martinez, Dave Pagan, and catcher Rick Dempsey to the Baltimore Orioles in exchange for pitchers Ken Holtzman, Doyle Alexander, Grant Jackson, Jimmy Freeman, and catcher Elrod Hendricks.

December 2, 1971
Yankees trade right-handed pitcher Stan Bahnsen to the Chicago White Sox in exchange for third baseman Rich McKinney.

November 26, 1986
Yankees trade pitchers Doug Drabek, Brian Fisher, and Logan Easley to the Pittsburgh Pirates for pitchers Rick Rhoden, Cecilio Guante, and Pat Clements.

March 28, 1986
Yankees trade designated hitter Don Baylor to the Boston Red Sox for designated hitter Mike Easler.

December 12, 1985
Yankees send catcher Ron Hassey and pitcher Joe Cowley to the Chicago White Sox for left-handed pitcher Britt Burns, minor league shortstop Mike Soper, and outfielder Glen Braxton.

Strangest Regular-Season Games in Yankees History

July 24, 1983 and August 18, 1983: Pine Tar and the Resumption

A most bizarre ending to a game that really didn't end for 25 days puts this one at the top of the list. With two out in the top of the ninth, the Yankees led the Kansas City Royals 4–3 and Goose Gossage faced his old nemesis, Hall of Famer George Brett, with the tying run at first.

Brett unloaded on a Gossage heater for a two-run bomb into the right-field stands and a 5–4 Royals lead, or so everyone thought.

Only a few weeks earlier, the Yankees had noticed that Brett's bat seemed to exceed the legal limit (18 inches) of pine tar, a sub-stance used for gripping the bat better. But Manager Billy Martin saved the appeal for a situation just like this one.

The umpires, led by crew chief Joe Brinkman, measured the amount of pine tar by placing Brett's bat alongside the flat surface at the top of home plate, which measures 17 inches wide. Brinkman said that "Brett's bat had heavy pine tar 19 or 20 inches from the tip of the handle."

Home-plate umpire Tim McClelland faced the Royals dugout and put up his right arm to signal that Brett would be called out for using an illegal bat. Brett's wild romp toward McClelland and the umpiring crew is one for the ages. At that moment, the bat that Brett used became the most valuable piece of merchandise on the planet. Security men whisked the bat away to where it could be examined by American League president Lee MacPhail. The Royals filed an offi-cial protest with the League office and on July 28, MacPhail announced his decision.

The bat used by George Brett in the infamous Pine Tar Game is immortalized in Cooperstown. Photo courtesy of MLB Photos via Getty Images.

After a short recap of the events, MacPhail concluded his opening statement by citing that "the rules do not provide that a hitter be called out for excessive use of pine tar." MacPhail went on to say, "The game becomes a suspended game at that point and must be completed." The teams took the field for one and one-third innings of baseball, and Kansas City preserved their 5–4 victory.

September 18, 1993: Fan Runs on Field to Give Yanks Second Chance to Beat Boston

With two out in the bottom of the ninth, and the Yankees trailing Boston 3–1, pinch-hitter Mike Stanley, who was the tying run at the plate, lifted what appeared to be a game-ending fly-out to left. Red Sox left fielder Mike Greenwell made the catch, but the game was not over. Third-base umpire Tim Welke had called time after a fan ran on the field from the third-base side.

Stanley took advantage of the gift by stroking a single to left to put two runners on. Wade Boggs followed with a single to make it 3–2. After a walk to Dion James loaded the bases, Don Mattingly drove home the tying and winning runs to give the Yankees a stunning victory over their arch rivals.

April 10, 1976: Game-Winning Grand Slam Is Not on the Money as Yanks Beat Milwaukee

It was only the second game of the season, but you could argue that it set a tone for what was to be a return to the top. The Yankees rallied for five runs in the top of the ninth to take a 9–6 lead over the Brewers at Milwaukee's County Stadium.

The Brew Crew had the bases loaded and nobody out with Don Money at the plate facing Yankees reliever Dave Pagan. Money hit an apparent game-winning grand slam, but first-base umpire Jim McKean had called time before the pitch was thrown, so the blow did not count.

Money flied harmlessly to right. After George Scott drove in a run with a sacrifice fly, left-hander Ken Brett was brought on to retire Darrell Porter on a ground-out to second for his first and only Yankees save.

Most Crushing Defeats in Yankees History

1. **October 13, 1960:** Bill Mazeroski's Series walk-off home run stuns Yanks
2. **October 20, 2004:** Red Sox win Game 7 to complete comeback from 3–0 ALCS deficit
3. **November 4, 2004:** Arizona rallies with two in the bottom of the ninth of Game 7 off Mariano Rivera to deny Yanks fourth-straight World Series championship
4. **October 8, 1995:** Yankees blow lead in deciding Game 5 to Seattle, who win on Edgar Martinez's walk-off double
5. **October 5, 1997:** Indians catcher Sandy Alomar Jr. homers off Rivera in eighth inning of Game 4 as Cleveland rallies to win the game and the Series the next day
6. **October 4, 1955:** Brooklyn's Johnny Podres shuts Yanks out in the seventh game at Yankee Stadium as the Dodgers win their first World Series after losing five times
7. **October 10, 1980:** George Brett's three-run homer off Goose Gossage leads Royals to a three-game sweep of the Yanks in the 1980 ALCS
8. **October 5, 1985:** Former Yankees pitcher Doyle Alexander eliminates Yanks from AL East race on the penultimate day of the season
9. **October 1, 1974:** Brewers eliminate Yanks from AL East race with 10th-inning, walk-off win in Milwaukee
10. **July 10, 1999:** Matt Franco's walk-off, two-run single off Mariano Rivera gives Mets stunning 9–8 win in the most dramatic finish of the Subway Series games

July 1, 1990: Hawkins Loses a No-Hitter and Then Loses No-Hitter Again

Yankees pitcher Andy Hawkins, who was struggling going into this game, thought he had regained his abilities to get hitters out as he took a no-hitter into the eighth inning against the White Sox in Chicago. Problem was, the Yankees were being shut out as well.

After retiring the first two hitters in the White Sox eighth, an error by Yankees third baseman Mike Blowers and two walks loaded the bases. Chisox third baseman Robin Ventura lifted a fly ball toward left field. Jim Leyritz dropped it, allowing three runs to score. A subsequent error allowed a fourth run to go home, and Hawkins was the loser in a 4–0 complete-game no-hitter, or so it was thought at the time.

A little more than a year later, the committee for statistical accuracy ruled that a no-hit game was one "in which a pitcher or pitchers complete a game of nine innings or more without allowing a hit." Hawkins's no-hit game was wiped off the books.

August 13, 1978: Yanks' Rally Takes Bird-Bath and Provokes a Rule Change

The Yankees trailed the Orioles 3–0 as they played the top of the seventh at Baltimore's Memorial Stadium through a steady rainfall. The Bombers scored five times to take a 5–3 lead, but a delay ensued and the umpiring crew waited 36 minutes to call the game.

According to the rule book, "the score reverts back to the last completed inning," so the Orioles were awarded a 3–0 victory, which prompted howls of protest from the Yankees side.

Head umpire Don Denkinger had declared the field unplayable, but the Yankees felt that Orioles manager Earl Weaver had manipulated things so that the game would go the Birds' way. "That little shrimp has these umpires intimidated," said Yankees left fielder Lou Piniella.

Two days prior, the umpires waited out a rain delay for two and a half hours before awarding a 2–1 win to the Yankees in five innings. The Orioles never batted in the bottom of the sixth, so the score reverted back to the end of five innings.

The irony of this bizarre event was that it prompted a rule change.

By the NUMBERS 19—The Yankees longest regular-season winning streak, which came during the 1947 season. It began on June 29 in the second game of a doubleheader against Washington, and it ended in Detroit on July 18.

In December 1978 the Baseball Rules Committee decided that instead of a game reverting back to the previous inning when postponed by rain, it will end at the exact time the umpire stops play. If the visiting team has scored to tie or take the lead, and the home team hasn't gotten up yet, the game will be suspended and picked up at that point.

TRIVIA

Can you name the Yankees pitcher who holds the franchise record by walking 13 batters in one game?

Answers to the trivia questions are on pages 186–187.

July 19, 1975: Bizarre Doubleheader Sees Yanks Win a Home Game on the Road—Munson Called Out for Using an Illegal Bat

One of the most bizarre days in Yankees history was played out at Minnesota's Metropolitan Stadium. It was a day that saw the Yankees wearing their road uniforms, yet they had the last licks and rallied for two runs in the bottom of the sixteenth to beat the Twins 8–7. The game was the completion of a suspended game at Shea Stadium on the day before the All-Star break, which was stopped by the American League curfew after 14 innings with the game tied at six.

Lou Piniella's single scored Chris Chambliss with the winning run as the Yankees scored a walk-off win in Minnesota. Left-hander Tippy Martinez, who was pitching in the minors when the game was suspended in New York, picked up the win in relief.

In the regulation game, Thurman Munson's RBI single was wiped out when home-plate umpire Art Frantz ruled that the Yankees captain's bat had an illegal amount of pine tar on it. Frantz called Munson out, but unlike the George Brett pine-tar incident, which was to occur exactly eight years and five days later, there was no ruling issued by the American League.

September 30, 1971: Yanks Win on Forfeit as Washington Fans Storm Field in Final Senators Game

The Yankees closed the 1971 season in Washington in what was to be the final game for the Senators. The team moved to Arlington, Texas, to become the Texas Rangers beginning with the 1972 campaign. A crowd of more than 14,000 was on hand to take in the final Senators' game at RFK Stadium.

Washington scored twice in the bottom of the eighth to take a 7–5 lead. Senators pitcher Joe Grzenda retired the first two Yankees hitters, and as Yankees second baseman Horace Clarke approached the plate for what could've been the final at-bat, fans began pouring onto the field in droves. The umpires waited for about five minutes and then decided to forfeit the game to the Yankees.

A number of derogatory signs lambasting the owner, Robert Short, were seen throughout the ballpark. The announcement of the forfeit was made over the public address system, but the crowd hardly reacted at all.

The game went into the books as a 9–0 forfeit, but the records do count, despite the fact that there was no winning or losing pitcher, because the Yankees were trailing when the forfeit occurred.

The Stadium: A Field of Dreams Whose Dreams Have Been Fulfilled

Stadium I

If you grew up outside of New York, to you this structure is one of the most famous buildings in the world. If you're from New York, you know it only as "The Stadium."

From the House That Ruth Built to the Cathedral of Baseball to the Big Ball Orchid in the South Bronx, this famous sports entity has carted many monikers. But the abundance of sports and cultural history that's been made at 161st Street and River Avenue in the Bronx is immeasurable.

Yankee Stadium was conceived in the minds of Colonels Jacob Ruppert and Tillinghast L'Hommedieu Huston, who owned the team in the early 1920s. But it nearly made its mark on the island of Manhattan instead of the Bronx.

The Yankees were sharing the Polo Grounds with the Giants, but that relationship broke down when the Yankees began drawing more fans due to Babe Ruth's presence. The club needed its own home field. Both owners were seriously considering a different site on which to build this colossal ballpark.

The two colonels were looking at a piece of land located between 136th and 138th Streets, near Broadway, but the Bronx area was larger and more comparable to the Polo Grounds, which stood on the other side of the Harlem River.

On February 5, 1921, the 10-acre site on the east bank of the river was chosen for the new home of the New York Yankees.

The Osborn Engineering Company of Cleveland, Ohio, was awarded the contract at a reported price of $2.5 million. It was hoped that the park would be ready sometime during the 1922 season, but circumstances prevented the construction from getting started on time. On March 31, 1922, the last hurdle was cleared and the work began on May 6.

After 284 working days, the stadium was ready to go for its inaugural game on April 18 versus Boston.

The day before, both teams worked out to get used to the new facility. It wasn't yet the House That Ruth Built, but the Babe himself was impressed during his first time standing on the field. "Looks pretty far out to that right-field fence," joked Ruth. After all, it was only 294 feet down the line in right, created solely for Ruth's benefit so that he would have an advantage in order to hit more home runs.

TRIVIA

On April 26, 2005, Alex Rodriguez hit three home runs and drove in 10 against the Angels. Which pitcher gave up all three home runs?

Answers to the trivia questions are on pages 186–187.

The dimensions were unlike anything ever seen before. The cavernous left-center field gap (aka "death valley") measured 500 feet. Center field was 487 feet while the right-center field gap was 350 feet. The numbers would change throughout the years, but the field would never lose its glory.

The magnificent design premiered with three concrete decks extending from behind home plate toward the corners. There was a single deck in left-center field, and the bleachers made up the remainder of the outfield.

The plan was to add a third deck in left-center field. In the winter of 1927–28, a second and third deck were added and some box seats were removed. The foul pole down the left-field line increased from 281 feet to 301 feet.

One of the most famous elements in the stadium was the façade that decorated the lining of the roof. It was made of copper, 15 feet deep, and it had such a melancholy look as it engulfed the top of the ballpark.

The first game was scheduled to start at 3:30 in the afternoon following a slew of opening ceremonies that included the raising of the 1922 American League championship flag. Additionally, the seventh regiment band led by the famous John Philip Sousa played the National Anthem. Then it was time to play ball.

When Yankees starting pitcher Bob Shawkey threw the first pitch to Boston's Chick Fewster, it was the start of many memorable moments to come.

Of course, what would an opening game at Ruth's house be without a four bagger from the man himself? Ruth obliged the more than 74,000 fans on hand with a three-run shot into the right-center field bleachers off the Sox's Howard Ehmke. And the Yanks were off and running.

Throughout the history of Stadium I, baseball was the main attraction, but sporting events such as championship boxing, NFL football with the New York Giants, and international soccer graced the grass of Yankee Stadium for many years. But the Yankees always starred on the marquee. Concerts, shows, and even a rodeo have been part of the agenda at the famous ballpark, not to mention an appearance by the pope—but the baseball history that has been written there is priceless.

Stadium I underwent changes to its appearance starting in 1928 when the triple deck grandstand in left field was extended beyond the foul pole. Right field was extended in 1937, which allowed for upper deck home runs from both sides. The famous auxiliary scoreboards that graced right- and left-center field and showed the line score of the game were built in the late 1940s. Death Valley was shortened from 500 feet to 490 feet for the second year of play. It was shortened again in 1937 to 457 feet, where it stayed for the stadium's final 39 years until the remodeling in 1976. Lights were added in 1946 while the first electronic message board debuted in 1959.

One of the early memories provided by the stadium backdrop was in September 1927 when Ruth hit his 60th home run off Washington's Tom Zachary.

July 4, 1939, was a historic afternoon at the stadium as Lou Gehrig orated his famous farewell speech before a packed house that had no knowledge of the fact that the Yankees legend would not live much longer.

Stadium I played host to 27 World Series and two All-Star Games, but it was more than just sports that enabled the great edifice to stand the test of time. Big events grazed the grass numerous times. When Joe Louis knocked out Germany's Max Schmeling in their famous rematch of 1938, it brought the stadium into the forefront of current events. It was the ultimate political statement that can only be made by a sporting event at a time when the country was three and a half years away from war.

"The Greatest Game Ever Played" was staged at Yankee Stadium. That's the phrase that was coined after the Baltimore Colts defeated the New York Giants in overtime, 23–17, in the 1958 NFL championship game. It was December 28, 1958, on a dreary winter day when NFL football burst into the forefront of the sporting public. The game was televised live and was widely credited for launching televised football into the mega-media outlet that it's become.

TRIVIA

Former Yankees pitcher Roger Clemens wore what number when he first played in New York?

Answers to the trivia questions are on pages 186–187.

One of the charms of Yankee Stadium I was the phenomenon of the monuments that stood in play in deep center field. Beginning in 1932, a total of three monuments were displayed in center field that paid tribute to Miller Huggins, Lou Gehrig, and Babe Ruth.

In August 1972 the Yankees signed a 30-year lease to play in a remodeled Yankee Stadium beginning in 1976. The final game at the original Yankee Stadium was played on September 30, 1973. Before an announced crowd of more than 32,000, the Yankees dropped an 8–5 decision to Detroit.

One of the many intriguing quirks to Yankee Stadium was that the fans were allowed to leave the ballpark by walking out under the center-field bleachers. This ritual took place for almost every game right up until the finale in 1973, but it did create some security problems. Some fans would bolt so quickly onto the field that they were able to interact with Mickey Mantle as he trotted in from center field after the final out was recorded.

Yankee Stadium historian Tony Morante recalled the formation of the Suicide Six. To keep the fans at bay, stadium ushers would form a "chorus line" around the rim of the field. The Suicide Six were six special ushers whose only priority was to escort Mantle off the field without any fan interference.

Stadium II

Two and a half calendar years after playing their last game in the Bronx, the Yankees returned to a new and refurbished Yankee Stadium on April 15, 1976. It was a successful reopening as the Yankees beat the Minnesota Twins 11–4.

It didn't take long for Stadium II to start weaving its own set of memories as the Yankees won the 1976 American League Pennant on a walk-off, series-winning home run from Yankees first baseman Chris Chambliss.

The first of three straight World Series to grace the "new" ballpark was a four-game sweep at the hands of the Cincinnati Reds, but the Yankees would rebound to win back-to-back World Series titles in 1977 and 1978.

The cavernous dimensions from the original Yankee Stadium were reduced somewhat. Left-center field, which was 457 feet, was shortened to 430 feet. Straight-away center went from 463 feet to 417 feet. In 1988 left-center field was reduced to 399 feet, and center field was reduced to 408 feet because the Yankees were a predominantly right-hand hitting club in those years.

Stadium II did not feature an NFL team, but some preseason games were played there. Concerts, championship fights, and soccer games also graced the field of Stadium II, but the Yankees continued to write their own, unique sports history.

Stadium II has already outdone Stadium I in one regard. There have already been two perfect games pitched at Stadium II, while there was only one pitched at the original park. The Yankees won 20 of their 26 World Series championships at Stadium I. The latter-day Yankees have won six World Series in 30 years at the remodeled place.

The Voice of Yankee Stadium

Yankee Stadium supplies its own brand of history every night when the most famous public-address announcer in the world opens his

An aerial view of "the House That Ruth Built," taken in 1996.

microphone. For the past 56 years, Bob Sheppard has announced the Yankees lineups with his own, unique style that has charmed baseball fans for generations. His omnipresent voice bellowing throughout the spacious ballpark has been a staple of Yankee Stadium since he debuted on April 17, 1951, as the Yankees hosted the Boston Red Sox in the season opener.

Since that time, Sheppard has announced 22 World Series and numerous playoff games, not to mention New York Giants football and pro soccer. Away from the ballpark, Sheppard has lent his famous voice to St. John's University basketball and football games.

The native New Yorker presented his microphone to the Baseball Hall of Fame in Cooperstown in 2000 and is a member of the New York Sports Hall of Fame. The longtime PA announcer has experienced many great moments, but he lists four baseball games and one football game as his most memorable: Don Larsen's perfect game in

1956; Roger Maris's 61st home run on the final day of the 1961 season; Reggie Jackson's three-home-run game to clinch the 1977 World Series; and getting to introduce President George W. Bush, who threw out the first ball before Game 3 of the 2001 World Series. The classic 1958 NFL title game between the Giants and Baltimore Colts that went into overtime was Sheppard's best football moment.

Sheppard has enthralled many a generation of fans throughout his fabulous career.

TRIVIA

Which player holds the Yankees single-season record for most sacrifice flies?

Answers to the trivia questions are on pages 186–187.

Stadium III

In June 2005 the Yankees announced plans for a brand-new Yankee Stadium to be built across the street from the site of the historic ballpark. The new Stadium will be a state-of-the-art facility that will combine modern comforts with a touch of nostalgia. An exterior façade that resembles the original Stadium will house an inner structure featuring five to six times more retail square footage than Stadium II. Reportedly, the dimensions will remain the same and the auxiliary scoreboards that graced the outfield gaps of the old ballpark will be restored in the new park. The stadium, which will seat 51,000, will not feature a three-deck look anymore. Instead, there will be 30,000 lower-tier seats with 20,000 in the upper tier. A restaurant will replace the black center-field bleachers with better access to Monument Park. The new ballpark is slated to open in 2009.

ANSWERS TO
TRIVIA QUESTIONS

Page 4: Andy Pettitte was the last Yankees rookie pitcher to win five games after September 1 (in 1995).

Page 6: Bernie Williams and Jorge Posada switch-hit home runs from both sides of the plate in the same game becoming the only duo to do so in major league history.

Page 12: John Elway, a member of the Pro Football Hall of Fame, was a second-round selection and the Yankees number one selection in 1981.

Page 17: d) When he made his major league debut, Derek Jeter wore No. 2.

Page 22: Lindy McDaniel was the last Yankees pitcher to hit a home run (in 1972).

Page 32: Mickey Mantle was an All-Star twice as a first baseman.

Page 35: No one has had career hit number 3,000 in a Yankees uniform.

Page 40: Gerald Williams (on May 1, 1996 at Camden Yards) holds the record for hits in a single game with six.

Page 44: Hank Bauer drove in the other run with an RBI single.

Page 55: Leo Durocher wore No. 7 in 1929 when the Yankees became the first team to make numbers a permanent part of their uniform.

Page 58: George Frazier was the Yankees pitcher who got the final out in the top of the ninth.

Page 80: Don Mattingly's number when he made his major league debut was No. 46.

Page 88: Earle Combs was the first Yankee to wear No. 1.

Page 113: Pete Vuckovich was the former Milwaukee Brewers pitcher who beat the Yankees in the 1981 division series and wore a Yankees uniform in the movie *Major League.*

Page 125: Paul O'Neill wore the pinstripes for two perfect games and two no-hitters.

Page 128: Clete Boyer moved to shortstop from third for the ninth inning of Game 7 of the 1960 World Series, and Joe DeMaestri, who replaced Tony Kubek the previous inning, moved to third.

Page 133: Hideki Matsui made the last out of the Houston Astros' six-pitcher, no-hitter in 2003.

Page 136: Willie Randolph has the record for walks drawn in one season by a right-handed hitter, with 119 walks in 1980.

Page 142: Alfonso Soriano wore No. 66 for nine games.

Page 167: Yogi Berra holds the Yankees career record for pinch-hit home runs with nine.

Page 169: Cliff Mapes wore Babe Ruth's No. 3 after Ruth left the Yankees and before it was retired in 1948.

Page 172: d) Mickey Mantle wore No. 6 when he broke in during the 1951 season.

Page 177: Tommy Byrne walked 13 batters in a 1949 game.

Page 180: Bartolo Colon gave up all three of Alex Rodriguez's home runs.

Page 182: Clemens wore No. 12 when he first played in New York.

Page 185: Roy White holds the Yankees single-season record for most sacrifice flies with 17 in 1971.

New York Yankees All-Time Roster (through 2006 season)

Listed players have appeared in at least one game as a New York Yankee. Those listed with an asterisk appeared in a game but did not play the field.

A

Jim Abbott (P)	1993–94
Harry Ables (P)	1911
Bobby Abreu (OF)	2006
Juan Acevedo (P)	2003
Spencer Adams (2B)	1926
Doc Adkins (P)	1903
Steve Adkins (P)	1990
Luis Aguayo (SS)	1988
Jack Aker (P)	1969–72
Mike Aldrete (OF)	1996
Doyle Alexander (P)	1976, 1982–83
Walt Alexander (C)	1915–17
Bernie Allen (2B)	1972–73
Johnny Allen (P)	1932–35
Neil Allen (P)	1985, 1987–88
Carlos Almanzar (P)	2001
Erick Almonte (SS)	2001, 2003
Sandy Alomar Sr. (2B)	1974–76
Felipe Alou (OF)	1971–73
Matty Alou (OF)	1973
Dell Alston (OF)	1977–78
Ruben Amaro (SS)	1966–68
Jason Anderson (P)	2003
John Anderson (OF)	1904–05
Rick Anderson (P)	1979
Ivy Andrews (P)	1931–32, 1937–38
Pete Appleton (P)	1933
Angel Aragon (3B)	1914, 1916–17
Rugger Ardizoia (P)	1947
Alex Arias (SS)	2002
Mike Armstrong (P)	1984–86
Brad Arnsberg (P)	1986–87
Luis Arroyo (P)	1960–63
Tucker Ashford (3B)	1981
Paul Assenmacher (P)	1993
Joe Ausanio (P)	1994–95
Jimmy Austin (3B)	1909–10
Chick Autry (C)	1924
Oscar Azocar (OF)	1990

B

Loren Babe (3B)	1952–53
Stan Bahnsen (P)	1966, 1968–71
Bill Bailey (OF)	1911
Frank Baker (3B)	1916–19, 1921–22
Frank Baker (SS)	1970–71
Steve Balboni (1B)	1981–83, 1989–90
Neal Ball (SS)	1907–09
Scott Bankhead (P)	1995
Willie Banks (P)	1997–98
Steve Barber (P)	1967–68
Jesse Barfield (OF)	1989–92
Cy Barger (P)	1906–07
Ray Barker (1B)	1965–67
Frank Barnes (P)	1930
Honey Barnes (C)	1926
Ed Barney (OF)	1915

George Batten (2B)	1912	Eddie Bockman (3B)	1946
Hank Bauer (OF)	1948–59	Ping Bodie (OF)	1918–21
Paddy Baumann (2B)	1915–17	Len Boehmer (1B)	1969, 1971
Don Baylor (OF)	1983–85	Brian Boehringer (P)	1995–97, 2001
Walter Beall (P)	1924–27	Wade Boggs (3B)	1993–97
T.J. Beam (P)	2006	Don Bollweg (1B)	1953
Colter Bean (P)	2005–06	Bobby Bonds (OF)	1975
Jim Beattie (P)	1978–79	Ricky Bones (P)	1996
Rich Beck (P)	1965	Ernie Bonham (P)	1940–46
Zinn Beck (3B)	1918	Juan Bonilla (2B)	1985, 1987
Fred Beene (P)	1972–74	Aaron Boone (3B)	2003
Joe Beggs (P)	1938	Luke Boone (2B)	1913–16
John Bell (OF)	1907	Frenchy Bordagaray (OF)	1941
Zeke Bella (OF)	1957	Rich Bordi (P)	1985, 1987
Mark Bellhorn (2B)	2005	Joe Borowski (P)	1997–98
Clay Bellinger (3B)	1999–2001	Hank Borowy (P)	1942–45
Benny Bengough (C)	1923–30	Babe Borton (1B)	1913
Juan Beniquez (OF)	1979	Daryl Boston (OF)	1994
Armando Benitez (P)	2003	Jim Bouton (P)	1962–68
Lou Berberet (C)	1954–55	Clete Boyer (3B)	1959–66
Dave Bergman (OF)	1975, 1977	Ryan Bradley (P)	1998
Juan Bernhardt (OF)	1976	Scott Bradley (C)	1984–85
Walter Bernhardt (P)	1918	Neal Brady (P)	1915, 1917
Dale Berra (SS)	1985–86	Darren Bragg (OF)	2001
Yogi Berra (C)	1946–63	Ralph Branca (P)	1954
Bill Bevens (P)	1944–47	Norm Branch (P)	1941–42
Monte Beville (C)	1903–04	Marshall Brant (1B)	1980
Harry Billiard (P)	1908	Garland Braxton (P)	1925–26
Doug Bird (P)	1980–81	Don Brennan (P)	1933
Ewell Blackwell (P)	1952–53	Jim Brenneman (P)	1965
Rick Bladt (OF)	1975	Ken Brett (P)	1976
Paul Blair (OF)	1977–80	Marv Breuer (P)	1939–43
Walter Blair (C)	1907–11	Billy Brewer (P)	1996
Johnny Blanchard (C)	1955, 1959–65	Fritzie Brickell (SS)	1958–59
Gil Blanco (P)	1965	Jim Brideweser (SS)	1951–53
Wade Blasingame (P)	1972	Marshall Bridges (P)	1962–63
Steve Blateric (P)	1972	Harry Bright (1B)	1963–64
Gary Blaylock (P)	1959	Ed Brinkman (SS)	1975
Curt Blefary (C)	1970–71	Johnny Broaca (P)	1934–37
Elmer Bliss (P)	1903–04	Lew Brockett (P)	1907, 1909, 1911
Ron Blomberg (1B)	1969, 1971–76	Jim Bronstad (P)	1959
Mike Blowers (3B)	1989–91	Tom Brookens (3B)	1989

Scott Brosius (3B)	1998–2001	Andy Cannizaro (SS)	2006
Bob Brower (OF)	1989	Robinson Cano (2B)	2005–06
Boardwalk Brown (P)	1914–15	Jose Canseco (OF)	2000
Bobby Brown (OF)	1946–52, 1954	Mike Cantwell (P)	1916
Bobby Brown (OF)	1979–81	Andy Carey (3B)	1952–60
Curt Brown (P)	1984	Roy Carlyle (OF)	1926
Hal Brown (P)	1962	Duke Carmel (OF)	1965
Jumbo Brown (P)	1932–33, 1935–36	Dick Carroll (P)	1909
Kevin Brown (P)	2004–05	Ownie Carroll (P)	1930
Brian Bruney (P)	2006	Tommy Carroll (SS)	1955–56
Jim Bruske (P)	1998	Chuck Cary (P)	1989–91
Billy Bryan (C)	1966–67	Hugh Casey (P)	1949
Jess Buckles (P)	1916	Alberto Castillo (C)	2002
Mike Buddie (P)	1998–99	Roy Castleton (P)	1907
Jay Buhner (OF)	1987–88	Bill Castro (P)	1981
Bill Burbach (P)	1969–71	Danny Cater (1B)	1970–71
Lew Burdette (P)	1950	Rick Cerone (C)	1980–84, 1987, 1990
Tim Burke (P)	1992	Bob Cerv (OF)	1951–56, 1960–62
George Burns (1B)	1928–29	Shawn Chacon (P)	2005–06
Alex Burr (OF)	1914	Chris Chambliss (1B)	1974–79, 1988
Ray Burris (P)	1979	Frank Chance (1B)	1913–14
Homer Bush (2B)	1997–98, 2004	Spud Chandler (P)	1937–47
Joe Bush (P)	1922–24	Les Channell (OF)	1910, 1914
Tom Buskey (P)	1973–74	Darrin Chapin (P)	1991
Ralph Buxton (P)	1949	Ben Chapman (P)	1930–36
Joe Buzas (SS)	1945	Mike Chartak (OF)	1940, 1942
Harry Byrd (P)	1954	Hal Chase (1B)	1905–13
Sammy Byrd (OF)	1929–34	Jack Chesbro (P)	1903–09
Tommy Byrne (P)	1943, 1946–51, 1954–57	Randy Choate (P)	2000–03
Marty Bystrom (P)	1984–85	Clay Christiansen (P)	1984
		Al Cicotte (P)	1957
C		Allie Clark (OF)	1947
Melky Cabrera (OF)	2005–06	George Clark (P)	1913
Greg Cadaret (P)	1989–92	Jack Clark (1B)	1988
Miguel Cairo (2B)	2004, 2006	Tony Clark (1B)	2004
Charlie Caldwell (P)	1925	Horace Clarke (2B)	1965–74
Ray Caldwell (P)	1910–18	Walter Clarkson (P)	1904–07
Johnny Callison (OF)	1972–73	Brandon Claussen (P)	2003
Howie Camp (OF)	1917	Ken Clay (P)	1977–79
Bert Campaneris (SS)	1983	Roger Clemens (P)	1999–2003
Archie Campbell (P)	1928	Pat Clements (P)	1987–88
John Candelaria (P)	1988–89	Tex Clevenger (P)	1961–62

Lu Clinton (OF)	1966–67	Joe Cowley (P)	1984–85
Al Closter (P)	1971–72	Bobby Cox (3B)	1968–69
Andy Coakley (P)	1911	Casey Cox (P)	1972–73
Jim Coates (P)	1956, 1959–62	Birdie Cree (OF)	1908–15
Jim Cockman (3B)	1905	Lou Criger (C)	1910
Rich Coggins (OF)	1975–76	Herb Crompton (C)	1945
Rocky Colavito (OF)	1968	Bubba Crosby (OF)	2004–06
King Cole (P)	1914–15	Frank Crosetti (SS)	1932–48
Curt Coleman (3B)	1912	Ivan Cruz (OF)	1997
Jerry Coleman (2B)	1949–57	Jose Cruz Sr. (OF)	1988
Michael Coleman (OF)	2001	Jack Cullen (P)	1962, 1965–66
Rip Coleman (P)	1955–56	Roy Cullenbine (OF)	1942
Bob Collins (C)	1944	Nick A. Cullop (P)	1916–17
Dave Collins (OF)	1982	Nick Cullop*	1926
Joe Collins (1B)	1948–57	John Cumberland (P)	1968–70
Orth Collins (P)	1904	Jim Curry (2B)	1911
Pat Collins (C)	1926–28	Chad Curtis (OF)	1997–99
Rip Collins (P)	1920–21	Fred Curtis (1B)	1905
Frank Colman (OF)	1946–47		
Jesus Colome (P)	2006	**D**	
Loyd Colson (P)	1970	Babe Dahlgren (1B)	1937–40
Earle Combs (OF)	1924–35	Bud Daley (P)	1961–64
David Cone (P)	1995–2000	Tom Daley (OF)	1914–15
Tom Connelly (OF)	1920–21	Johnny Damon (OF)	2006
Joe Connor (C)	1905	Bert Daniels (OF)	1910–13
Wid Conroy (3B)	1903–08	Bobby Davidson (P)	1989
Jose Contreras (P)	2003–04	Chili Davis (OF)	1998–99
Andy Cook (P)	1993	George Davis (P)	1912
Doc Cook (OF)	1913–16	Kiddo Davis (OF)	1926
Dusty Cooke (OF)	1930–32	Lefty Davis (SS)	1903
Ron Coomer (1B)	2002	Ron Davis (P)	1978–81
Johnny Cooney (P)	1944	Russ Davis (3B)	1994–95
Phil Cooney (3B)	1905	Brian Dayett (OF)	1983–84
Don Cooper (P)	1985	John Deering (P)	1903
Guy Cooper (P)	1914	Jim Deidel (C)	1974
Dan Costello (OF)	1913	Ivan DeJesus (SS)	1986
Henry Cotto (OF)	1985–87	Frank Delahanty (OF)	1905–06, 1908
Ensign Cottrell (P)	1915	Wilson Delgado (2B)	2000
Clint Courtney (C)	1951	Bobby DelGreco (OF)	1957–58
Ernie Courtney (1B)	1903	David Dellucci (OF)	2003
Stan Coveleski (P)	1928	Jim Delsing (OF)	1949–50
Billy Cowan (OF)	1969	Joe DeMaestri (SS)	1960–61

Ray Demmitt (OF)	1909
Rick Dempsey (C)	1973–76
Bucky Dent (SS)	1977–82
Jorge DePaula (P)	2003–05
Claud Derrick (SS)	1913
Russ Derry (OF)	1944–45
Jim Deshaies (P)	1984
Jimmie DeShong (P)	1934–35
Orestes Destrade (1B)	1987
Charlie Devens (P)	1932–34
Al DeVormer (C)	1921–22
Bill Dickey (C)	1928–43, 1946
Murry Dickson (P)	1958
Joe DiMaggio (OF)	1936–42, 1946–51
Kerry Dineen (OF)	1975–76
Craig Dingman (P)	2000
Art Ditmar (P)	1957–61
Sonny Dixon (P)	1956
Pat Dobson (P)	1973–75
Cozy Dolan (3B)	1911–12
Atley Donald (P)	1938–45
Mike Donovan (3B)	1908
Wild Bill Donovan (P)	1915–16
Brian Dorsett (OF)	1989–90
Octavio Dotel (P)	2006
Rich Dotson (P)	1988–89
Patsy Dougherty (OF)	1904–05
John Dowd (SS)	1912
Al Downing (P)	1961–69
Brian Doyle (2B)	1978–80
Jack Doyle (1B)	1905
Slow Joe Doyle (P)	1906–10
Doug Drabek (P)	1986
Bill Drescher (C)	1944–46
Karl Drews (P)	1946–48
Monk Dubiel (P)	1944–45
Joe Dugan (3B)	1922–28
Mariano Duncan (2B)	1996–97
Ryne Duren (P)	1958–61
Leo Durocher (SS)	1925, 1928–29
Cedric Durst (OF)	1927–30

E

Mike Easler (OF)	1986–87
Rawly Eastwick (P)	1978
Doc Edwards (C)	1965
Foster Edwards (P)	1930
Robert Eenhoorn (2B)	1994–96
Dave Eiland (P)	1988–91, 1995
Darrell Einertson (P)	2000
Kid Elberfeld (SS)	1903–09
Gene Elliott (OF)	1911
Dock Ellis (P)	1976–77
John Ellis (C)	1969–72
Kevin Elster (SS)	1994–95
Alan Embree (P)	2005
Red Embree (P)	1948
Clyde Engle (OF)	1909–10
Jack Enright (P)	1917
Todd Erdos (P)	1998–2000
Roger Erickson (P)	1982–83
Felix Escalona (SS)	2004–05
Juan Espino (C)	1982–83, 1985–86
Alvaro Espinoza (2B)	1988–91
Bobby Estalella (C)	2001
Nick Etten (1B)	1943–46
Barry Evans (2B)	1982

F

Charles Fallon*	1905
Steve Farr (P)	1991–93
Doc Farrell (SS)	1932–33
Sal Fasano (C)	2006
Alex Ferguson (P)	1918, 1921, 1925
Frank Fernandez (C)	1967–69
Tony Fernandez (SS)	1995
Mike Ferraro (3B)	1966, 1968
Wes Ferrell (P)	1938–39
Tom Ferrick (P)	1950–51
Chick Fewster (OF)	1917–22
Cecil Fielder (1B)	1996–97
Mike Figga (C)	1997–99
Ed Figueroa (P)	1976–80
Pete Filson (P)	1987

Happy Finneran (P)	1981	Milt Gaston (P)	1924
Mike Fischlin (SS)	1986	Mike Gazella (3B)	1923, 1926–28
Brian Fisher (P)	1985–86	Joe Gedeon (2B)	1916–17
Gus Fisher (C)	1912	Lou Gehrig (1B)	1923–39
Ray Fisher (P)	1910–17	Bob Geren (C)	1988–91
Mike Fitzgerald (OF)	1911	Al Gettel (P)	1945–46
John Flaherty (C)	2003–05	Jason Giambi (1B)	2002–06
Tim Foli (SS)	1984	Joe Giard (P)	1927
Ray Fontenot (P)	1983–84	Jake Gibbs (C)	1962–71
Barry Foote (C)	1981–82	Paul Gibson (P)	1993–94, 1996
Ben Ford (P)	2000	Sam Gibson (P)	1930
Edward "Whitey" Ford (P)	1950, 1953–67	Frank Gilhooley (OF)	1913–18
Russ Ford (P)	1909–13	Charles Gipson (OF)	2003
Tony Fossas (P)	1999	Joe Girardi (C)	1996–99
Eddie Foster (SS)	1910	Fred Glade (P)	1908
Jack Fournier (1B)	1918	Frank Gleich (OF)	1919–20
Andy Fox (2B)	1996–97	Joe Glenn (C)	1932–33, 1935–38
Ray Francis (P)	1925	Lefty Gomez (P)	1930–42
Wayne Franklin (P)	2005	Jessie Gonder (C)	1960–61
George Frazier (P)	1981–83	Fernando Gonzalez (2B)	1974
Mark Freeman (P)	1959	Pedro Gonzalez (1B)	1963–65
Ray French (SS)	1920	Wilbur Good (P)	1905
Lonny Frey (2B)	1947–48	Dwight Gooden (P)	1996–97, 2000
Bob Friend (P)	1966	Art Goodwin (P)	1905
John Frill (P)	1910	Joe Gordon (2B)	1938–43, 1946
Bill Fulton (P)	1987	Tom Gordon (P)	2004–05
Dave Fultz (OF)	1903–05	Tom Gorman (P)	1952–54
Liz Funk (OF)	1929	Rich Gossage (P)	1978–83, 1989
		Dick Gossett (C)	1913–14
G		Larry Gowell (P)	1972
John Gabler (P)	1959–60	Alex Graman (P)	2004–05
Joe Gallagher (OF)	1939	Wayne Granger (P)	1973
Mike Gallego (2B)	1992–94	Ted Gray (P)	1955
Oscar Gamble (OF)	1976, 1979–84	Eli Grba (P)	1959–60
John Ganzel (1B)	1903–04	Nick Green (2B)	2006
Mike Garbark (C)	1944–45	Paddy Greene (SS)	1903
Damaso Garcia (2B)	1978–79	Todd Greene (C)	2001
Karim Garcia (OF)	2002, 2003	Ken Griffey Sr. (OF)	1982–86
Billy Gardner (2B)	1961–62	Mike Griffin (P)	1979–81
Earle Gardner (2B)	1908–12	Clark Griffith (P)	1903–07
Rob Gardner (P)	1970–72	Bob Grim (P)	1954–58
Ned Garvin (P)	1904	Burleigh Grimes (P)	1934

Oscar Grimes (3B)	1943–46	Roy Hartzell (OF)	1911–16
Jason Grimsley (P)	1999–2000	Buddy Hassett (1B)	1942
Lee Grissom (P)	1940	Ron Hassey (C)	1985–86
Johnny Grobowski (C)	1927–29	Andy Hawkins (P)	1989–91
Buddy Groom (P)	2005	Chicken Hawks (OF)	1921
Cecilio Guante (P)	1987–88	Charlie Hayes (3B)	1992, 1996–97
Lee Guetterman (P)	1988–92	Fran Healy (C)	1976–78
Ron Guidry (P)	1975–88	Mike Heath (C)	1978
Aaron Guiel (OF)	2006	Neal Heaton (P)	1993
Brad Gulden (C)	1979–80	Don Heffner (2B)	1934–37
Don Gullett (P)	1977–78	Mike Hegan (1B)	1964, 1965–67,
Bill Gullickson (P)	1987		1973–74
Randy Gumpert (P)	1946–48	Fred Heimach (OF)	1928–29
Larry Gura (P)	1974–75	Woodie Held (SS)	1954, 1957
		Charlie Hemphill (OF)	1908–11
H		Rollie Hemsley (C)	1942–44
John Habyan (P)	1990–93	Bill Henderson (P)	1930
Bump Hadley (P)	1936–40	Rickey Henderson (OF)	1985–89
Kent Hadley (1B)	1960	Harvey Hendrick (OF)	1923–24
Ed Hahn (OF)	1905–06	Elrod Hendricks (C)	1976–77
Noodles Hahn (P)	1906	Tim Hendryx (OF)	1915–17
Hinkey Haines (OF)	1923	Sean Henn (P)	2005
George Halas (OF)	1919	Tommy Henrich (OF)	1937–42, 1946–50
Bob Hale (1B)	1961	Bill Henry (P)	1966
Jimmie Hall (OF)	1969	Drew Henson (3B)	2002–03
Mel Hall (OF)	1989–92	Felix Heredia (P)	2003–04
Brad Halsey (P)	2004	Adrian Hernandez (P)	2001–02
Roger Hambright (P)	1971	Leo Hernandez (3B)	1986
Steve Hamilton (P)	1963–70	Michel Hernandez (C)	2003
Chris Hammond (P)	2003	Orlando Hernandez (P)	1998–2002, 2004
Mike Handiboe (OF)	1911	Xavier Hernandez (P)	1994
Jim Hanley (P)	1913	Ed Herrmann (C)	1975
Truck Hannah (C)	1918–20	Hugh High (OF)	1915–16
Ron Hansen (SS)	1970–71	Oral Hildebrand (P)	1939–40
Harry Hanson (C)	1913	Glenallen Hill (OF)	2000
Jim Hardin (P)	1971	Jesse Hill (OF)	1935
Bubbles Hargrave (C)	1930	Shawn Hillegas (P)	1992
Harry Harper (P)	1921	Frank Hiller (P)	1946, 1948–49
Toby Harrah (3B)	1984	Mack Hillis (2B)	1924
Greg Harris (P)	1994	Rich Hinton (P)	1972
Joe Harris (OF)	1914	Sterling Hitchcock (P)	1992–95,
Jim Ray Hart (OF)	1973–74		2001–03

Myril Hoag (OF)	1931–32, 1934–38
Butch Hobson (3B)	1982
Red Hoff (P)	1911–13
Danny Hoffman (P)	1906–07
Solly Hofman (OF)	1916
Fred Hofmann (C)	1919–25
Bill Hogg (P)	1905–08
Bobby Hogue (P)	1951–52
Ken Holcombe (P)	1945
Bill Holden (OF)	1913–14
Al Holland (P)	1986–87
Ken Holloway (P)	1930
Darren Holmes (P)	1998
Fred Holmes (1B)	1903
Roger Holt (2B)	1980
Ken Holtzman (P)	1976–78
Rick Honeycutt (P)	1995
Don Hood (P)	1979
Wally Hood (P)	1949
Johnny Hopp (1B)	1950–52
Shags Horan (OF)	1924
Ralph Houk (C)	1947–54
Elston Howard (C)	1955–67
Matt Howard (2B)	1996
Steve Howe (P)	1991–96
Harry Howell (P)	1903
Jay Howell (P)	1982–84
Dick Howser (SS)	1967–68
Waite Hoyt (P)	1921–30
Rex Hudler (2B)	1984–85
Charlie Hudson (P)	1987–88
Keith Hughes (OF)	1987
Long Tom Hughes (P)	1904
Tom Hughes (P)	1906–07, 1909–10
John Hummel (OF)	1918
Mike Humphreys (OF)	1991–93
Ken Hunt (OF)	1959–60
Billy Hunter (SS)	1955–56
Jim "Catfish" Hunter (P)	1975–79
Mark Hutton (P)	1993–94, 1996
Ham Hyatt (OF)	1918

I

Pete Incaviglia (OF)	1997
Hideki Irabu (P)	1997–99

J

Fred Jacklitsch (C)	1905
Grant Jackson (P)	1976
Reggie Jackson (OF)	1977–81
Dion James (OF)	1992–93, 1995–96
Johnny James (P)	1958, 1960–61
Stan Javier (OF)	1984
Domingo Jean (P)	1993
Stanley Jefferson (OF)	1989
Jackie Jensen (OF)	1950–52
Mike Jerzembeck (P)	1998
Derek Jeter (SS)	1995–2006
Elvio Jimenez (OF)	1964
D'Angelo Jiminez (3B)	1999
Brett Jodie (P)	2001
Tommy John (P)	1979–82, 1986–89
Alex Johnson (OF)	1974–75
Billy Johnson (3B)	1943, 1946–51
Cliff Johnson (C)	1977–79
Darrell Johnson (C)	1957–58
Deron Johnson (3B)	1960–61
Don Johnson (P)	1947, 1950
Ernie Johnson (SS)	1923–25
Hank Johnson (P)	1925–26, 1928–32
Jeff Johnson (P)	1991–93
Johnny Johnson (P)	1944
Ken Johnson (P)	1969
Lance Johnson (OF)	2000
Nick Johnson (1B)	2001–03
Otis Johnson (SS)	1911
Randy Johnson (P)	2005–06
Roy Johnson (OF)	1936–37
Russ Johnson (OF)	2005
Jay Johnstone (OF)	1978–79
Darryl Jones (OF)	1979
Gary Jones (P)	1970–71
Jimmy Jones (P)	1989–90
Ruppert Jones (OF)	1980

Sad Sam Jones (P)	1922–26	Ron Klimkowski (P)	1969–70, 1972
Tim Jordan (1B)	1903	Steve Kline (P)	1970–74
Arndt Jorgens (C)	1929–39	Mickey Klutts (SS)	1976–78
Felix Jose (OF)	2000	Bill Knickerbocker (SS)	1938–40
Jeff Juden (P)	1999	Brandon Knight (P)	2001–02
Mike Jurewicz (P)	1965	John Knight (SS)	1909–11, 1913
David Justice (OF)	2000–01	Chuck Knoblauch (2B)	1998–2001
		Mark Koenig (SS)	1925–30
K		Jim Konstanty (P)	1954–56
Jim Kaat (P)	1979–80	Andy Kosco (OF)	1968
Scott Kamieniecki (P)	1991–96	Steve Kraly (P)	1953
Bob Kammeyer (P)	1978–79	Jack Kramer (P)	1951
Frank Kane*	1919	Ernie Krueger (C)	1915
Bill Karlon (OF)	1930	Dick Kryhoski (1B)	1949
Herb Karpel (P)	1946	Tony Kubek (SS)	1957–65
Steve Karsay (P)	2002–05	Johnny Kucks (P)	1955–59
Jeff Karstens (P)	2006	Bill Kunkel (P)	1963
Benny Kauff (OF)	1912	Bob Kuzava (P)	1951–54
Curt Kaufman (P)	1982–83		
Eddie Kearse (C)	1942	**L**	
Ray Keating (P)	1912–16, 1918	Joe Lake (P)	1908–09
Bob Keefe (P)	1907	Bill Lamar (OF)	1917–19
Willie Keeler (OF)	1903–09	Hal Lanier (SS)	1972–73
Randy Keisler (P)	2000–01	Dave LaPoint (P)	1989–90
Mike Kekich (P)	1969–73	Frank LaPorte (3B)	1905–10
Charlie Keller (OF)	1939–43, 1945–49, 1952	Dave LaRoche (P)	1981–83
Pat Kelly (2B)	1991–97	Don Larsen (P)	1955–59
Roberto Kelly (OF)	1987–92, 2000	Lyn Lary (SS)	1929–34
Steve Kemp (OF)	1983–84	Chris Latham (OF)	2003
John Kennedy (SS)	1967	Marcus Lawton (OF)	1989
Jerry Kenney (3B)	1967, 1969–72	Matt Lawton (OF)	2005
Matt Keough (P)	1983	Gene Layden (OF)	1915
Jimmy Key (P)	1993–96	Tony Lazzeri (2B)	1926–37
Steve Kiefer (3B)	1989	Tim Leary (P)	1990–92
Dave Kingman (OF)	1977	Ricky Ledee (OF)	1998–2000
Harry Kingman (1B)	1914	Travis Lee (1B)	2004
Fred Kipp (P)	1960	Joe Lefevbre (OF)	1980
Frank Kitson (P)	1907	Al Leiter (P)	1987–89, 2005
Ron Kittle (OF)	1986–87	Mark Leiter (P)	1990
Ted Kleinhans (P)	1936	Frank Leja (1B)	1954–55
Red Kleinow (C)	1904–10	Jack Lelivelt (OF)	1912–13
Ed Klepfer (P)	1911, 1913	Eddie Leon (SS)	1975

Louis LeRoy (P)	1905–06
Ed Levy (OF)	1942, 1944
Duffy Lewis (OF)	1919–20
Jim Lewis (P)	1982
Terry Ley (P)	1971
Jim Leyritz (C)	1990–96,
	1999–2000
Cory Lidle (P)	2006
Jon Lieber (P)	2004
Ted Lilly (P)	2000–02
Paul Lindblad (P)	1978
Johnny Lindell (P)	1941–50
Phil Linz (SS)	1962–65
Bryan Little (2B)	1986
Jack Little (OF)	1912
Clem Llewellyn (P)	1922
Graeme Lloyd (P)	1996–98
Esteban Loaiza (P)	2004
Gene Locklear (OF)	1976–77
Kenny Lofton (OF)	2004
Sherm Lollar (C)	1947–48
Tim Lollar (P)	1980
Phil Lombardi (OF)	1986–87
Dale Long (1B)	1960, 1962–63
Herman Long (SS)	1903
Terence Long (OF)	2006
Ed Lopat (P)	1948–55
Art Lopez (OF)	1965
Hector Lopez (OF)	1959–66
Baldy Louden (3B)	1907
Slim Love (P)	1916–18
Torey Lovullo (3B)	1991
Mike Lowell (3B)	1998
Johnny Lucadello (2B)	1947
Joe Lucey (2B)	1920
Roy Luebbe (C)	1925
Matt Luke (DH)	1996
Jerry Lumpe (3B)	1956–59
Scott Lusader (OF)	1991
Sparky Lyle (P)	1972–78
Al Lyons (P)	1946–47
Jim Lyttle (OF)	1969–71

M

Duke Maas (P)	1958–61
Kevin Maas (1B)	1990–93
Bob MacDonald (P)	1995
Danny MacFayden (P)	1932–34
Ray Mack*	1947
Tommy Madden*	1910
Elliott Maddox (OF)	1974–76
Dave Madison (P)	1950
Lee Magee (OF)	1916–17
Sal Maglie (P)	1957–58
Stubby Magner (SS)	1911
Jim Magnuson (P)	1973
Fritz Maisel (3B)	1913–17
Hank Majeski (3B)	1946
Frank Makosky (P)	1937
Pat Malone (P)	1935–37
Pat Maloney (OF)	1912
Al Mamaux (P)	1924
Rube Manning (P)	1907–10
Mickey Mantle (OF)	1951–68
Jeff Manto (1B)	1999
Josias Manzanillo (P)	1995
Cliff Mapes (OF)	1948–51
Roger Maris (OF)	1960–66
Cliff Markle (P)	1915–16, 1924
Jim Marquis (P)	1925
Armando Marsans (OF)	1917–18
Cuddles Marshall (P)	1946, 1948–49
Sam Marsonek (P)	2004
Billy Martin (2B)	1950–53, 1955–57
Hersh Martin (OF)	1944–45
Jack Martin (SS)	1912
Tino Martinez (1B)	1996–2001, 2005
Tippy Martinez (P)	1974–76
Jim Mason (SS)	1974–76
Vic Mata (OF)	1984–85
Hideki Matsui (OF)	2003–06
Don Mattingly (1B)	1982–95
Carlos May (OF)	1976–77
Rudy May (P)	1974–76, 1980–83
John Mayberry (1B)	1982

Carl Mays (P)	1919–23	Andy Messersmith (P)	1978
Lee Mazzilli (OF)	1982	Tom Metcalf (P)	1963
Larry McCall (P)	1977–78	Bud Metheny (OF)	1943–46
Joe McCarthy (C)	1905	Hensley Meulens (OF)	1989–93
Pat McCauley (C)	1903	Bob Meusel (OF)	1920–29
Larry McClure (OF)	1910	Bob Meyer (P)	1964
George McConnell (P)	1909, 1912–13	Dan Miceli (P)	2003
Mike McCormick (P)	1970	Gene Michael (SS)	1968–74
Lance McCullers (P)	1989–90	Ezra Midkiff (3B)	1912–13
Lindy McDaniel (P)	1968–73	Pete Mikkelsen (P)	1964–65
Mickey McDermott (P)	1956	Larry Milbourne (SS)	1981–83
Danny McDevitt (P)	1961	Sam Militello (P)	1992–93
Dave McDonald (1B)	1969	Bill Miller (P)	1952–54
Donzell McDonald (OF)	2001	Elmer Miller (OF)	1915–18, 1921–22
Jim McDonald (P)	1952–54	John Miller (OF)	1966
Gil McDougald (SS)	1951–60	Alan Mills (P)	1990–91
Jack McDowell (P)	1995	Buster Mills (OF)	1940
Sam McDowell (P)	1973–74	Mike Milosevich (SS)	1944–45
Lou McEvoy (P)	1930–31	Paul Mirabella (P)	1979
Herm McFarland (OF)	1903	Willie Miranda (SS)	1953–54
Andy McGaffigan (P)	1981	Bobby Mitchell (OF)	1970
Lynn McGlothen (P)	1982	Fred Mitchell (P)	1910
Bob McGraw (P)	1917–20	Johnny Mitchell (SS)	1921–22
Deacon McGuire (C)	1904–07	Johnny Mize (1B)	1949–53
Marty McHale (P)	1913–15	Kevin Mmahat (P)	1989
Irish McIllveen (OF)	1908–09	George Mogridge (P)	1915–20
Tim McIntosh (3B)	1996	Dale Mohorcic (P)	1988–89
Bill McKechnie (2B)	1913	Fenton Mole (1B)	1949
Rich McKinney (3B)	1972	Bill Monbouquette (P)	1967–68
Frank McManus (C)	1904	Raul Mondesi (OF)	2002–03
Norm McMillan (OF)	1922	Ed Monroe (P)	1917–18
Tommy McMillan (SS)	1912	Zack Monroe (P)	1958–59
Mike McNally (3B)	1921–24	John Montefusco (P)	1983–86
Herb McQuaid (P)	1926	Rich Monteleone (P)	1990–93
George McQuinn (1B)	1947–48	Archie Moore (OF)	1964–66
Bobby Meacham (SS)	1983–88	Earl Moore (P)	1907
Charlie Meara (OF)	1914	Wilcy Moore (P)	1927–29, 1932–33
Jim Mecir (P)	1996–97	Ray Morehart (2B)	1927
George Medich (P)	1972–75	Omar Moreno (OF)	1983–85
Bob Melvin (C)	1994	Mike Morgan (P)	1982
Ramiro Mendoza (P)	1996–2002, 2005	Tom Morgan (P)	1951–52, 1954–56
Fred Merkle (1B)	1925–26	George Moriarty (3B)	1906–08

Jeff Moronko (OF)	1987	Harry Niles (2B)	1908
Hal Morris (1B)	1988–89	C.J. Nitkowski (P)	2004
Ross Moschitto (OF)	1965, 1967	Otis Nixon (OF)	1983
Jerry Moses (C)	1973	Matt Nokes (C)	1990–94
Terry Mulholland (P)	1994	Irv Noren (OF)	1952–56
Charlie Mullen (2B)	1914–16	Don Nottebart (P)	1969
Jerry Mumphrey (OF)	1981–83	Les Nunamaker (C)	1914–17
Bob Muncrief (P)	1951		
Bobby Munoz (P)	1993	**O**	
Thurman Munson (C)	1969–79	Johnny Oates (C)	1980–81
Bobby Murcer (OF)	1965–66,	Mike O'Berry (C)	1984
	1969–74, 1979–83	Andy O'Connor (P)	1908
Johnny Murphy (P)	1932,	Jack O'Connor (C)	1903
	1934–43, 1946	Paddy O'Connor (C)	1918
Rob Murphy (P)	1994	Heinie Odom (3B)	1925
Dale Murray (P)	1983–85	Lefty O'Doul (P)	1919–20, 1922
George Murray (P)	1922	Rowland Office (OF)	1983
Larry Murray (OF)	1974–76	Bob Ojeda (P)	1994
Mike Mussina (P)	2001–06	Rube Oldring (OF)	1905, 1916
Mike Myers (P)	2006	John Olerud (1B)	2004
		Bob Oliver (1B)	1975
N		Joe Oliver (C)	2001
Jerry Narron (C)	1979	Nate Oliver*	1969
Dan Naulty (P)	1999	Paul O'Neill (OF)	1993–2001
Dioner Navarro (C)	2004	Steve O'Neill (C)	1925
Denny Neagle (P)	2000	Jesse Orosco (P)	2003
Bots Nekola (P)	1929	Queenie O'Rourke (OF)	1908
Gene Nelson (P)	1981	Al Orth (P)	1904–09
Jeff Nelson (P)	1996–2000, 2003	Donovan Osborne (P)	2004
Luke Nelson (P)	1919	Champ Osteen (3B)	1904
Graig Nettles (3B)	1973–83	Joe Ostrowski (P)	1950–52
Tex Neuer (P)	1907	Antonio Osuna (P)	2003
Ernie Nevel (P)	1950–51	Bill Otis (OF)	1912
Floyd Newkirk (P)	1934	Stubby Overmire (P)	1951
Bobo Newsom (P)	1947	Spike Owen (SS)	1993
Doc Newton (P)	1905–09		
Gus Niarhos (C)	1946, 1948–50	**P**	
Joe Niekro (P)	1985–87	John Pacella (P)	1982
Phil Niekro (P)	1984–85	Del Paddock (3B)	1912
Jerry Nielsen (P)	1992	Juan Padilla (P)	2004
Scott Nielsen (P)	1986, 1988–89	Dave Pagan (P)	1973–76
Wil Nieves (C)	2005	Joe Page (P)	1944–50

Mike Pagliarulo (3B)	1984–89	Bob Porterfield (P)	1948–51
Donn Pall (P)	1994	Jorge Posada (C)	1995–2006
Christian Parker (P)	2001	Scott Pose (OF)	1997
Clay Parker (P)	1989–90	Jack Powell (P)	1904–05
Ben Paschal (OF)	1924–29	Jake Powell (OF)	1936–40
Dan Pasqua (OF)	1985–87	Mike Powers (1B)	1905
Gil Patterson (P)	1977	Del Pratt (2B)	1918–20
Jeff Patterson (P)	1995	Jerry Priddy (3B)	1941–42
Mike Patterson (OF)	1981–82	Curtis Pride (OF)	2003
Carl Pavano (P)	2005	Johnnie Priest (2B)	1911–12
Dave Pavlas (P)	1995–96	Bret Prinz (P)	2003–04
Monte Pearson (P)	1936–40	Scott Proctor (P)	2004–06
Roger Peckinpaugh (SS)	1913–21	Alfonso Pulido (P)	1986
Steve Peek (P)	1941	Ambrose Puttman (P)	1903–05
Hipolito Pena (P)	1988		
Herb Pennock (P)	1923–33	**Q**	
Joe Pepitone (1B)	1962–69	Paul Quantrill (P)	2004–05
Marty Perez (3B)	1977	Mel Queen (P)	1942, 1944, 1946–47
Melido Perez (P)	1992–95	Ed Quick (P)	1903
Pascual Perez (P)	1990–91	Jack Quinn (P)	1909–12, 1919–21
Robert Perez (OF)	2001	Jamie Quirk (C)	1989
Cecil Perkins (P)	1967		
Cy Perkins (C)	1931	**R**	
Gaylord Perry (P)	1980	Tim Raines (OF)	1996–98
Fritz Peterson (P)	1966–74	Dave Rajsich (P)	1978
Andy Pettitte (P)	1995–2003	Bobby Ramos (C)	1982
Ken Phelps (1B)	1988–89	Domingo Ramos (SS)	1978
Andy Phillips (1B)	2004–06	John Ramos (C)	1991
Eddie Phillips (C)	1932	Pedro Ramos (P)	1964–65
Jack Phillips (1B)	1947–49	Lenny Randle (OF)	1979
Cy Pieh (P)	1913–15	Willie Randolph (2B)	1976–88
Bill Piercy (P)	1917, 1921	Vic Raschi (P)	1946–53
Duane Pillette (P)	1949–50	Dennis Rasmussen (P)	1984–87
Lou Piniella (OF)	1974–84	Darrell Rasner (P)	2006
George Pipgras (P)	1923–24, 1927–33	Shane Rawley (P)	1982–84
Wally Pipp (1B)	1915–25	Jeff Reardon (P)	1994
Jim Pisoni (OF)	1959–60	Jack Reed (OF)	1961–63
Eric Plunk (P)	1989–91	Jimmie Reese (2B)	1930–31
Dale Polley (P)	1996	Kevin Reese (OF)	2005–06
Luis Polonia (OF)	1989–90, 1994–95, 2000	Hal Reniff (P)	1961–67
		Bill Renna (OF)	1953
Sidney Ponson (P)	2006	Tony Rensa (C)	1933

Roger Repoz (OF)	1964–66
Rick Reuschel (P)	1981
Dave Revering (1B)	1981–82
Al Reyes (P)	2003
Allie Reynolds (P)	1947–54
Bill Reynolds (C)	1913–14
Rick Rhoden (P)	1987–88
Gordon Rhodes (P)	1929–32
Harry Rice (OF)	1930
Bobby Richardson (2B)	1955–66
Nolen Richardson (SS)	1935
Branch Rickey (C)	1907
Dave Righetti (P)	1979, 1981–90
Jose Rijo (P)	1984
Danny Rios (P)	1997
Juan Rivera (OF)	2001–03
Mariano Rivera (P)	1995–2006
Ruben Rivera (OF)	1995–96
Mickey Rivers (OF)	1976–79
Phil Rizzuto (SS)	1941–42, 1946–56
Roxey Roach (SS)	1910–11
Dale Roberts (P)	1967
Andre Robertson (SS)	1981–85
Gene Robertson (3B)	1926–29
Aaron Robinson (C)	1943, 1945–47
Bill Robinson (OF)	1967–69
Bruce Robinson (C)	1979–80
Eddie Robinson (1B)	1954–56
Hank Robinson (P)	1918
Jeff Robinson (P)	1990
Alex Rodriguez (3B)	2004–06
Aurelio Rodriguez (3B)	1980–81
Carlos Rodriguez (SS)	1991
Eddie Rodriguez (2B)	1982
Ellie Rodriguez (C)	1968
Felix Rodriguez (P)	2005
Henry Rodriguez*	2001
Gary Roenicke (OF)	1986
Oscar Roettger (P)	1923–24
Jay Rogers (C)	1914
Kenny Rogers (P)	1996–97
Tom Rogers (P)	1921

Jim Roland (P)	1972
Red Rolfe (3B)	1931, 1934–42
Buddy Rosar (C)	1939–42
Larry Rosenthal (OF)	1944
Steve Roser (P)	1944–46
Braggo Roth (OF)	1921
Jerry Royster (3B)	1987
Muddy Ruel (C)	1917–20
Dutch Ruether (P)	1926–27
Red Ruffing (P)	1930–42, 1945–46
Allan Russell (P)	1915–19
Marius Russo (P)	1939–43, 1946
Babe Ruth (OF)	1920–34
Blondy Ryan (SS)	1935
Rosy Ryan (P)	1928

S

Johnny Sain (P)	1951–55
Lenn Sakata (3B)	1987
Mark Salas (C)	1987
Jack Saltzgaver (3B)	1932, 1934–37
Billy Sample (OF)	1985
Celerino Sanchez (3B)	1972–73
Rey Sanchez (2B)	1997, 2005
Deion Sanders (OF)	1989–90
Roy Sanders (P)	1918
Scott Sanderson (P)	1991–92
Charlie Sands*	1967
Fred Sanford (P)	1949–51
Rafael Santana (SS)	1988
Don Savage (3B)	1944–45
Rick Sawyer (P)	1974–75
Steve Sax (2B)	1989–91
Ray Scarborough (P)	1952–53
Germany Schaefer (OF)	1916
Harry Schaeffer (P)	1952
Roy Schalk (2B)	1932
Art Schallock (P)	1951–55
Wally Schang (C)	1921–25
Bob Schmidt (C)	1965
Butch Schmidt (P)	1909
Johnny Schmitz (P)	1952–53

Pete Schneider (P)	1919	Ruben Sierra (OF)	1995–96, 2003–05
Dick Schofield (SS)	1966	Charlie Silvera (C)	1948–56
Paul Schreiber (P)	1945	Dave Silvestri (SS)	1992–95
Art Schult*	1953	Ken Silvestri (C)	1941, 1946–47
Al Schulz (P)	1912–14	Hack Simmons (2B)	1912
Don Schulze (P)	1989	Dick Simpson (OF)	1969
Pius Schwert (C)	1914–15	Harry Simpson (OF)	1957–58
Everett Scott (SS)	1922–25	Duke Sims (C)	1973–74
George Scott (1B)	1979	Bill Skiff (C)	1926
Rodney Scott (SS)	1982	Camp Skinner (OF)	1922
Rod Scurry (P)	1985–86	Joel Skinner (C)	1986–88
Scott Seabol*	2001	Lou Skizas*	1956
Ken Sears (C)	1943	Bill Skowron (1B)	1954–62
Bob Seeds (OF)	1936	Roger Slagle (P)	1979
Kal Segrist (2B)	1952	Don Slaught (C)	1988–89
Fernando Seguignol (1B)	2003	Enos Slaughter (OF)	1954–59
George Selkirk (OF)	1934–42	Aaron Small (P)	2005–06
Ted Sepkowski*	1947	Roy Smalley (SS)	1982–84
Hank Severeid (C)	1926	Walt Smallwood (P)	1917, 1919
Joe Sewell (3B)	1931–33	Charley Smith (3B)	1967–68
Howard Shanks (3B)	1925	Elmer Smith (OF)	1922–23
Billy Shantz (C)	1960	Joe Smith (C)	1913
Bobby Shantz (P)	1957–60	Keith Smith (SS)	1984–85
Bob Shawkey (P)	1915–27	Klondike Smith (OF)	1912
Spec Shea (P)	1947–49, 1951	Lee Smith (P)	1993
Al Shealy (P)	1928	Matt Smith (P)	2006
George Shears (P)	1912	Harry Smythe (P)	1934
Tom Sheehan (P)	1921	J.T. Snow (1B)	1992
Gary Sheffield (OF)	2004–06	Eric Soderholm (3B)	1980
Rollie Sheldon (P)	1961–62, 1964–65	Luis Sojo (2B)	1996–99,
Skeeter Shelton (OF)	1915		2000–01, 2003
Roy Sherid (P)	1929–31	Tony Solaita (1B)	1968
Pat Sheridan (OF)	1991	Alfonso Soriano (2B)	1999–2003
Dennis Sherrill (SS)	1978, 1980	Steve Souchock (1B)	1946, 1948
Ben Shields (P)	1924–25	Jim Spencer (1B)	1978–81
Steve Shields (P)	1988	Shane Spencer (OF)	1998–2002
Bob Shirley (P)	1983–87	Charlie Spikes (OF)	1972
Urban Shocker (P)	1916–17, 1925–28	Russ Springer (P)	1992
Tom Shopay (OF)	1967, 1969	Bill Stafford (P)	1960–65
Ernie Shore (P)	1919–20	Jake Stahl (OF)	1908
Bill Short (P)	1960	Roy Staiger (3B)	1979
Norm Siebern (1B)	1956, 1958–59	Tuck Stainback (OF)	1942–45

Gerry Staley (P)	1955–56	Dick Tettelbach*	1955
Charley Stanceu (P)	1941, 1946	Bob Tewksbury (P)	1986–87
Andy Stankiewicz (2B)	1992–93	Marcus Thames (OF)	2002
Fred Stanley (SS)	1973–80	Ira Thomas (C)	1906–07
Mike Stanley (C)	1992–95, 1997	Lee Thomas*	1961
Mike Stanton (P)	1997–2002, 2005	Myles Thomas (P)	1926–29
Dick Starr (P)	1947–48	Stan Thomas (P)	1977
Dave Stegman*	1982	Gary Thomasson (OF)	1978
Dutch Sterrett (OF)	1912–13	Homer Thompson (C)	1912
Bud Stewart (OF)	1948	Kevin Thompson (OF)	2006
Lee Stine (P)	1938	Ryan Thompson (OF)	2000
Kelly Stinnett (C)	2006	Tommy Thompson (P)	1912
Snuffy Stirnweiss (2B)	1943–50	Jack Thoney (3B)	1904
Tim Stoddard (P)	1986–88	Hank Thormahlen (P)	1917–20
Mel Stottlemyre (P)	1964–74	Marv Throneberry (1B)	1955, 1958–59
Hal Stowe (P)	1960	Mike Thurman (P)	2002
Darryl Strawberry (OF)	1995–99	Luis Tiant (P)	1979–80
Gabby Street (C)	1912	Dick Tidrow (P)	1974–79
Marlin Stuart (P)	1954	Bobby Tiefenauer (P)	1965
Bill Stumpf (SS)	1912–13	Eddie Tiemeyer (1B)	1909
Tom Sturdivant*	1955–59	Ray Tift (P)	1907
Johnny Sturm (1B)	1941	Bob Tillman (C)	1967
Tanyon Sturtze (P)	2004–06	Thad Tillotson (P)	1967–68
Bill Sudakis (1B)	1974	Dan Tipple (P)	1915
Steve Sundra (P)	1936, 1938–40	Wayne Tolleson (SS)	1986–90
Dale Sveum (3B)	1998	Earl Torgeson (1B)	1961
Ed Sweeney (C)	1908–15	Rusty Torres (OF)	1971–72
Ron Swoboda (OF)	1971–73	Mike Torrez (P)	1977
		Cesar Tovar (OF)	1976
T		Bubba Trammell (OF)	2003
Fred Talbot (P)	1966–69	Tom Tresh (OF)	1961–69
Vito Tamulis (P)	1934–35	Gus Triandos (C)	1953–54
Frank Tanana (P)	1993	Steve Trout (P)	1987
Jesse Tannehill (P)	1903	Virgil Trucks (P)	1958
Tony Tarasco (OF)	1999	Frank Truesdale (P)	1914
Danny Tartabull (OF)	1992–95	Bob Turley (P)	1955–62
Wade Taylor (P)	1991	Chris Turner (C)	2000
Zack Taylor (C)	1934	Jim Turner (P)	1942–45
Frank Tepedino (OF)	1967, 1969–72		
Walt Terrell (P)	1989	**U**	
Ralph Terry (P)	1956–57, 1959–64	George Uhle (P)	1933–34
Jay Tessmer (P)	1998–2000, 2002	Tom Underwood (P)	1980–81

Bob Unglaub (3B)	1904	Pete Ward (1B)	1970
Cecil Upshaw (P)	1974	Jack Warhop (P)	1908–15
		George Washburn (P)	1941
V		Claudell Washington (OF)	1986–88, 1990
Elmer Valo (OF)	1960	Gary Waslewski (P)	1970–71
Russ Van Atta (P)	1933–35	Allen Watson (P)	1999–2000
Dazzy Vance (P)	1915, 1918	Bob Watson (1B)	1980–82
Joe Vance (P)	1937–38	Roy Weatherly (OF)	1943, 1946
John Vander Wal (OF)	2002	David Weathers (P)	1996–97
Bobby Vaughn (2B)	1909	Jeff Weaver (P)	2002–03
Hippo Vaughn (P)	1908, 1910–12	Jim Weaver (P)	1931
Javier Vazquez (P)	2004	Dave Wehrmeister (P)	1981
Bobby Veach (OF)	1925	Lefty Weinert (P)	1931
Randy Velarde (SS)	1987–95, 2001	David Wells (P)	1997–98,
Otto Velez (OF)	1973–76		2002–03
Mike Vento (OF)	2005	Ed Wells (P)	1929–32
Robin Ventura (3B)	2002–03	Butch Wensloff (P)	1943, 1947
Jose Veras (P)	2006	Julie Wera (3B)	1927, 1929
Joe Verbanic (P)	1967–68, 1970	Bill Werber (SS)	1930. 1933
Frank Verdi (SS)	1953	Dennis Werth (1B)	1979–81
Sammy Vick (OF)	1917–20	Jake Westbrook (P)	2000
Ron Villone (P)	2006	John Wetteland (P)	1995–96
Jose Vizcaino (2B)	2000	Stefan Wever (P)	1982
		Steve Whitaker (OF)	1966–68
W		Gabe White (P)	2003–04
Jake Wade (P)	1946	Rondell White (OF)	2002
Dick Wakefield*	1950	Roy White (OF)	1965–79
Jim Walewander (2B)	1990	Wally Whitehurst (P)	1996
Curt Walker (OF)	1919	George Whiteman (OF)	1913
Dixie Walker (OF)	1931, 1933–36	Mark Whiten (OF)	1997
Mike Wallace (P)	1974–75	Terry Whitfield (OF)	1974–76
Jimmy Walsh (OF)	1914	Ed Whitson (P)	1985–86
Joe Walsh (C)	1910–11	Kemp Wicker (P)	1936–38
Roxy Walters (C)	1915–18	Al Wickland (OF)	1919
Danny Walton (OF)	1971	Bob Wickman (P)	1992–96
Paul Waner*	1944–45	Chris Widger (C)	2002
Chien-Ming Wang (P)	2005–06	Bob Wiesler (P)	1951, 1954–55
Jack Wanner (SS)	1909	Bill Wight (P)	1946–47
Pee Wee Wanninger (SS)	1925	Ted Wilborn (OF)	1980
Aaron Ward (SS)	1917–26	Ed Wilkinson (OF)	1911
Gary Ward (OF)	1987–89	Bernie Williams (OF)	1991–2006
Joe Ward (2B)	1909	Bob Williams (C)	1911–13

Gerald Williams (OF)	1992–96, 2001–02	Dick Woodson (P)	1974
Harry Williams (1B)	1913–14	Hank Workman (1B)	1950
Jimmy Williams (2B)	1903–07	Jaret Wright (P)	2005–06
Stan Williams (P)	1963–64	Ken Wright (P)	1974
Todd Williams (P)	2001	Yats Wuestling (SS)	1930
Walt Williams (OF)	1974–75	John Wyatt (P)	1968
Archie Wilson (OF)	1951–52	Butch Wynegar (C)	1982–86
Enrique Wilson (3B)	2001–04	Jimmy Wynn (OF)	1977
George Wilson (OF)	1956		
Pete Wilson (P)	1908–09	**Y**	
Snake Wiltsie (P)	1903	Ed Yarnall (P)	1999–2000
Gordie Windhorn (OF)	1959	Joe Yeager (P)	1905–06
Dave Winfield (OF)	1981–90	Jim York (P)	1976
Jay Witasick (P)	2001	Curt Young (P)	1992
Mickey Witek*	1949	Ralph Young (SS)	1913
Mike Witt (P)	1990–91, 1993		
Whitey Witt (OF)	1922–25	**Z**	
Mark Wohlers (P)	2001	Tom Zachary (P)	1928–30
Barney Wolfe (P)	1903–04	Jack Zalusky (C)	1903
Harry Wolter (P)	1910–13	George Zeber (2B)	1977–78
Harry Wolverton (3B)	1912	Rollie Zeider (SS)	1913
Dooley Womack (P)	1966–68	Todd Zeile (1B)	2003
Tony Womack (2B)	2005	Guy Zinn (OF)	1911–12
Gene Woodling (OF)	1949–54	Bill Zuber (P)	1943–46
Ron Woods (OF)	1969–71	Paul Zuvella (SS)	1986–87